# LITTLE TOM DRENNAN

*By the same Author*

THE LIFE AND TIMES OF MARY ANN MCCRACKEN.

1770-1866

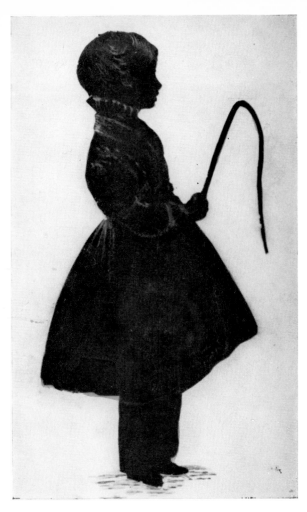

PLATE I: THOMAS HAMILTON DRENNAN.

*b.* 24 *March,* 1801, *d.* 25 *February,* 1812.

# Little
# Tom Drennan

## PORTRAIT OF A
## GEORGIAN CHILDHOOD

by

Mary McNeill

Dublin

THE DOLMEN PRESS

1962

*Printed and published at the Dolmen Press,
23 Upper Mount Street, Dublin 2,
in the Republic of Ireland.*

\*

*Distributed outside Ireland by
the Oxford University Press*

In gratitude to
the late Mrs. Adam Duffin
for her care of
the Drennan Letters.

# Contents

# ILLUSTRATIONS

# Introduction

The Georgian era is rich in its diaries and collections of personal letters from which the adult life of the period can be reconstructed. Rarer in that age—or indeed in any other—are personal records regarding the day-to-day life of children. It is, therefore, with more than ordinary delight that we gaze on the portrait of one particular child—little Tom Drennan—as it is displayed before us in the pages of the *Drennan Letters*. For what we have there *is* a veritable portrait, drawn by an artist's pen with a penetration and comprehension entirely beyond the scope of any artist's brush. Tom lived for long periods of time with his aunt, Mrs. M'Tier, in Belfast, and in the letters that passed between this aunt and her brother, Dr. William Drennan [Tom's father], in Dublin, every nuance and detail of the child's character is depicted—his incredible charm, his precociousness, his sense of fun, his naughtiness and, perhaps most engaging of all, his amazing delight in giving pleasure. Moreover, the portrait is not static, it lives; before our eyes the child grows physically and develops mentally over a sweep of eight short years.

Anyone familiar with *Pet Marjorie* will instantly discover points of resemblance between these two remarkable children. Marjorie Fleming [1803-1811] was born two years later than Thomas Hamilton Drennan, and died just three months earlier. Both were precocious: at seven years Pet Marjorie could recite long passages from Shakespeare and Swift, and Tom, as we shall see, entertained his friends by declaiming from *Henry IV* when he was only three. Both of them adored stories, went to parties in sedan chairs, probed with childish imaginings the problems of religion, used naughty words in fits of temper, but above all, possessed that 'power of affection'—to quote Dr. John Brown's phrase—which in the one case utterly captivated Sir Walter Scott, and in the other case, less notable, but no less ardent, devotees.

This is not the place to pursue comparisons, or to draw conclusions, but only to point out that whereas we depend on one short—though famous—essay for all we know about Pet Marjorie, a wealth of information is available regarding Little Tom. Here we have all about his upbringing, his education, his ailments and the way they were treated, the things that gave him pleasure and the incidents that made him sad, so that through the story of this one particular, dearly-loved, child we can form some idea of the attitude, in the middle class of society, towards children in general during the first decade of the nineteenth century.

Thomas Drennan was born in Dublin, lived most of his short life in Belfast and spent one long holiday in Shropshire. He had many and varied experiences, and the narrative provides countless points of practical interest for those who to-day, in any capacity, are interested in the care and education of children. Both his father and his aunt were inimitable letter-writers and I have told the story almost entirely in their words, words that, incidentally, reveal with the utmost clarity their own differing characteristics.

It was the late Mrs. Adam Duffin of Belfast, herself a granddaughter of Dr. William Drennan, who, with the help of her daughters, arranged and dated the entire collection of over 1,500 letters that passed between her grandfather and her great aunt from 1776-1819. This collection is now known as the *Drennan Letters* and has been deposited in the Northern Ireland Public Records Office. From the Misses Duffin, I have received the most generous help. I gratefully acknowledge their permission to quote from the *Drennan Letters*, and from another short series of letters from Dr. Drennan to his wife, still in their possession. It is to them that I am indebted for the use of all the illustrations—except that of the White Linen Hall—and, in addition, for much incidental information that contributes so greatly to 'the feel' of the situation.

Sometime towards the middle of the nineteenth century Cabin Hill, the little cottage so central to this story, was pulled down to give place to a spacious Victorian residence. The original name was retained. To-day the property has been engulfed, but mercifully not greatly mutilated, by the sprawling city of Belfast, the Victorian residence is a preparatory boarding school for boys, and many potential sixth-formers play in the grounds where once 'little Tom Drennan' was so happy.

Belfast.
1962.

# LITTLE TOM DRENNAN

# Chapter I : His first two years

LITTLE TOM DRENNAN was born in one of the high Georgian houses in Marlborough Street,* Dublin, on March 24th, 1801. He was the eldest child of Dr. William Drennan and of his wife Sarah [née Swanwick] who, the previous year, had come from her home in Shropshire to marry the now middle-aged physician — already renowned as the United Irishman successfully defended by John Philpot Curran on a charge of sedition; as an able pamphleteer; and as a poet of some merit.

The Drennan family belonged to Belfast, where the doctor's father had been minister of one of the two presbyterian churches, and where his mother and two sisters still resided. When this story opens one of the sisters, Mrs. Martha M'Tier — her christian name shortened to Matty — was a childless widow, energetic, forthright and immensely practical. Twelve years older than her brother, there existed between them an unusually strong attachment which, since Dr. Drennan's college days in Glasgow and Edinburgh, had found expression in the long and fascinating correspondence known now as the *Drennan Letters*. In due course the doctor had settled in Dublin where he practised as an *accoucheur*. Time passed, and as the early thirties bore down on her bachelor brother Mrs. M'Tier's letters begin to contain pressing suggestions as to a wife. When, eventually, the hand of Sarah Swanwick was won, she welcomed her sister-in-law with genuine delight and warm affection.

---

*No. 33.

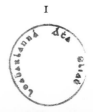

But, important though marriage was, it did nothing to
stop, or indeed to interrupt, the flow of letters: on they go,
concerned with politics, current affairs, literary criticism,
family news, local gossip, more than a touch of philoso-
phizing, the only difference being that now it was a triangular
affair, with Sarah contributing occasionally, but more frequently being addressed by Matty. The birth of the first
baby was awaited in Belfast with hardly less happy and tense
anticipation than in Dublin, and thereafter the correspondence adds nursery details to its list of contents. Mrs. M'Tier
finds, and sends, a nursemaid to Dublin; the child's name—
Thomas Hamilton Drennan—is chosen with approval from
all sides, and, in spite of the fact that the baby's father was
a doctor, various methods of feeding are advocated over
many weeks: 'This yelping cur of yours,' writes Matty, 'is
in my opinion *starved*. What objections have you to panada,
the food all get and all agree with. . . . You talk of many
giving advice, surely then the child is not well and by your
giving it cow's milk and water in the morning I fear the
nurse has not sufficient milk. Between you both I fear the
infant will be famished. . . . All *I* venture to recommend is
that *on him* you will not practise new-fangled experiments.'[1]
That final caustic remark probably referred to inoculation
against small-pox, for Dr. Drennan was one of the earliest
and most determined advocates of this form of protection,
and, in spite of anything that his sister might say, he writes
to her as follows when his son was two months old:

*We inoculated our Little Thomas on Tuesday before last,
and on last Tuesday he sickened, has been considerably
feverish until this morning, Friday, when it is I think,
much abated. The Eruption has appeared and I don't
believe he will have many small pocks; there appear about
thirty on his face, and as many on the rest of his Body,
except his arm which will be very sore, but there is no*

*unfavorable sign. . . . The weather has been favorable
while he was feverish, and he has at that time been
exposed freely to the air, with evident benefit. . . . When
the fever goes off entirely there is no danger. I shall be
glad it is over, as the S.pox is prevalent here and I got the
infection at a small distance in the Street. . . . He begins
to smile, and coo, as he did before. They say nothing so
uniform and unvary'd as an infant's countenance, but I
can count at least a dozen of miniature passions which shift
across it.*[2]

One is horrified to think of the risks that were run and the
suffering that was inflicted, while this preventive measure
was being perfected.

As the months passed Mrs. M'Tier longed to see her
nephew: 'Perhaps sometime you could spare a son,' she
writes wistfully, knowing that Sarah's second child would be
born before Thomas' first birthday. And again, 'I stop all
the young children I meet and inquire their age, that I might
bring his size (at least) to my view.'[3] A remark which makes
us realise how dependent we have since become on the art of
the photographer—amateur or professional.

There are frequent references to childish ailments. When
Tom was six months old his father writes:

*Thomas has cut a tooth and will soon show another, which
is an aera in the annals of this house.* [This tooth will be
mentioned again.] *We bought Betty a shawl on the occasion. The child has had a cough for some time which is not
very severe and may proceed from teething, but I have
judged it prudent to suspend the use of his morning cold
bath* [at six months!] *as independent of his cough he is
delicate & thin, but tall for his age.*[4]

Later—Tom is still 'delicate', but he can walk with only
'the slightest assistance of a finger to support him.' Some

weeks spent in the country, with his nurse-maid Betty, had
proved so beneficial that on his return home his father planned to 'send him and Betty thrice a week to Clontarf* on
one of the jaunting cars for the purpose of bathing.'[5] Certainly Dr. Drennan was a great believer in fresh air and
spartan training, but these constant references to delicate
health alarmed Mrs. M'Tier. Infant mortality might, in
general, be accepted with as little questioning as a high birth
rate; their own father, as she all too soon had occasion to
remind her brother, 'took 10 to the grave'[6]—and five had
been baby boys. But nothing must happen to this treasured
first-born son, and in her great anxiety Matty makes repeated
suggestions that the child should be sent from the supposedly
polluted air of the city to the purer atmosphere of Belfast—
or better still to Cabin Hill, the little cottage, three or four
miles distant, where two elderly relatives lived.

*I think myself* [she writes] *that at Cabin Hill there is
everything conducive to health, a house where two old
ladies are constantly resident & three servants . . . no
water* [pond] *or dangerous spot about the place. In town
he should be my companion Day & Night, I never Dine
abroad or go into company till after his bedtime & I have
two servants that would delight in him. . . . Doctor
Mateer† at my Door, and now* never *from home. Our
streets improved and safe, my hand could conduct him
daily the short road of affection to his G.Mother, who wd.
yet rejoice & be cheered by his visit. But still, so far from
urging,* I do not request it. *It would be a pang to you both,
& if anything sh'd happen him, regret in future and to
me misery. But if any circumstances, convenient or the*

---

* On the north side of Dublin Bay, now part of the city of Dublin.

† Her brother-in-law.

*reverse, sh'd tempt you to send him down, be assured I
shall rejoice in it, & that to me, never a slave to any fear,
he will be the object of new and interesting Hope.*[7]

At last, after months had passed and several plans had
been made and abandoned, it was agreed that Mrs. M'Tier
should go to Dublin to fetch the darling nephew.
Three months in a change of air would, in all probability, do
Tom good, and to have one child less in the house at that
particular moment would be easier for everyone, for Sarah
was now awaiting her third confinement. To prepare his
sister for the two-year-old Tom, Dr. Drennan writes:

*He is of a sociable, talkative disposition, and whenever he
is at his meals, all that are about him must take a little in
their turn, as he puts the spoon round and will not taste it
himself till his turn comes, which shows at least the command he has over his appetite, if not the strength of his
affections.*[8]

Something must now be said about the various relations
who awaited the little visitor in Belfast.

There was, first of all, his Grandmother, old Mrs. Drennan, then in her 87th year. She lived in the Parade, the
recently developed and fashionable district, facing the White
Linenhall. In her day she had been a forceful personage,
and even at this advanced age was able to provide congenial
entertainment for her friends—she 'had three card tables a
few nights ago, and out-sat some old buck at the Whist table.
She has sat in her Drawingroom all the summer' and was
enjoying 'your favorite Plutarch'. Nevertheless, her health
was failing, and she was cared for by her second daughter
Ann, or Nancy, a quiet, retiring person, totally unlike her
forthright sister. Mrs. M'Tier had a house of her own
nearby, but spent much of her time at Cabin Hill, the little
country cottage occupied by an elderly, and comparatively

affluent cousin, Miss Martha Young. Another cousin, Miss Bigger—Ann Jane—resided there too, both of them more or less invalids.

Mrs. M'Tier was the centre of this purely feminine circle. She was, at the opening of this story, sixty years of age, accounted then a much more advanced time of life than it is to-day, but there was nothing elderly about her outlook or the workings of her mind. Her married life had been short but very happy, and the memory of her husband, Samuel, was never far away. Her portrait—taken in earlier days—shows a fine face and suggests a resolute personality, but writing to her brother in connection with the proposed visit to Dublin, she paints this unflattering, but lively, self-portrait:

> *I wd. prepare you for meeting me, either here or in Dub:*
> *this spring, a little, pale, bleer eyed, broad, vulgarised old*
> *woman, but never in better spirits, having no sentimental*
> *fears or hopes, and very willing to enjoy the present even*
> *a little better than the matter, people & times permit.*[9]

She had, however, been careful to preface these remarks with the assertion that 'any mind I had (so far as I can judge) remains yet in its vigour, and unchanged; my temper I have taken pains to improve before trials made it still a harder task, and hope I have succeeded'.

Whatever her looks, she moved in the best society and had many friends and interests. With her husband she had been deeply involved in both the literary and political aspects of the liberal movement that flourished in Belfast at the close of the eighteenth century; Samuel M'Tier had held an important position in the United Irishmen and, in furtherance of her own humanitarian principles, Matty had been closely connected with a school for destitute girls, which provided a simple education and prepared them for domestic service. At her husband's death she had been left in straitened circumstances, and currency inflation, consequent on the long drawn-out war with France, played its customary havoc with a small fixed income. Still, she had many resources within herself, she was an ardent card-player, and a critical theatre-goer, delighting in the company of Mrs. Siddons when that most distinguished actress visited Belfast on several occasions.

Cabin Hill and its garden she loved. Though now owned by Miss Young, Matty and her husband had built it in accordance with the romantic vogue of the day for a country 'cabbin': together they had laid out the garden, and every stick and stone was dear to her. Her delight in all young life emphasises the pent up sorrow, long borne, that she had had no children of her own. In one letter there is this poignant sentence:

> *Every young thing, to the very trees & plants, attracts me so much that I feel it was mercy in Heaven not to make me a parent; in this I can acknowledge its goodness; but the harder lesson of allowing it, if I had been robbed of them I fear wd. have been beyond me. Yet, everything is borne, that is certain.*[10]

Instead of 'every young thing' she was surrounded by age and the infirmities of age, and it is not difficult to imagine how she longed to see her brother's child—'the bud of promise'—to use her own tender description of him. That he would eventually take such possession of her heart may, perhaps, have surprised even her.

So, on an April day in 1803 she set off for Dublin, 120 miles by coach, full of excitement in spite of her sixty years, and after a happy stay in Marlborough Street of only ten days—intended primarily as an opportunity for the child to become acquainted with his aunt—she undertook, unaided and completely undaunted, the return journey to Belfast with Thomas on her knee. What follows is her own descrip-tion of it, and any who have had occasion to carry off a two-year-old from his home surroundings will appreciate the skill with which she handled the ticklish situation.

> *Dear Sarah* [she writes]
>
> *I hope you were aware that you could not hear from me before Monday, indeed I intended writing when we got to Dundalk where we arrived at* 10 *o'c* [p.m.] *after the Mail had left. Your little darling was all animated delight the whole way, without regret for the past or fear for the future. . . . He committed himself to every chambermaid we met, & spent some minutes alone with each of them to their mutual satisfaction. The first good bed-chamber he entered he cried "Mama" but no more. At Dundalk I got him some warm bread & milk, the former he rejected, but drank the milk with so much pleasure I weaned him from it by a leg of boiled chicken & then we retired to a poor room & bad little bed for the night. I striped him, after which he very deliberately put on his little frock & his hat on his head declaring in a pritty firm tone he wd. not sleep in that room. I feared to debate—undress'd myself, steped into bed & told him I was going to put out the candle, on which he joined me for the night—an indifferent one to him and an entire sleepless one to me.*

There were many travellers in the hotel, so Mrs. M'Tier, 'determined to get the start of them', was off in a chaise by 5.45 next morning! They breakfasted at Newry, changed at Lisburn to a coach with four horses, and reached Belfast at 4 p.m., altogether a two-day journey. Instead of a weary, fractious child, Tom was 'intoxicated with delight'. A meal of stewed veal and beef steaks awaited them, 'the old Miss Mateers immediately came in, and, as the Table was high fed him, which he repaid by affability and smiles which to strangers astonished them'. He was then conducted 'the short road of affection' to his Grandmother. Being a little before their time Matty 'intended', as a delightful surprise for the old lady, 'that the child should walk in of himself while I stood at the Door, but Nancy had spied us out of the Window & met us with open arms & looks of approbation on the stairs, ushering us into my poor Mother's room, who was very unwell & in her bed'. It was surely an understatement to declare that such an introduction 'was a trial to Tom. He advanced reluctantly, gave her his hand, over which she wept & we staid to tea. He walked home between Nancy and me and he pointed immediately to the right door.'

Again there was the difficulty of bed-time:

*He would not go to sleep without my being in the bed. I thought the best method I knew was to tell him a long story about his Grandmother & it had the usual effect, and we both had a good night.*

Next day 'the novelty of everything charmed him: the bird [her parrot] awoke him, he listen'd to the Cock, and on my drawing the foot curtain and desiring him to look at the picture [*facing p.* 16] he did so for a moment, then cried "Papa" & resting his finger on his cheek, laughed heartily'. What an adorable child!

The following day Tom was taken to Cabin Hill to see Cousin Young. 'Her also he found in bed and did not relish it, tho' I was thankful he did not cry. Here he found in some corner, no one knew how, liquorice ball, with which he made himself such a figure it served as an excuse to get off. When he came home he received Dr. Mateer & other company with perfect good breeding, bore a barking little Dog & admired a cat and Kittens.' He then went to tea with his grandmother, and Nancy

*had to carry him back, owing, as I found when putting him to bed, to gravel that got into his shoes. He went to bed without me, for I found him likely to insist on my constant attendance. . . . Now I have given you every particular, a* dirty *tho' natural trick that happened at Lisburn\* excepted, when the child was pent up & would go from me with a pretty boy who caught his attention— for which he endured a washing without a murmur!*

Thus ends Matty's description of little Tom Drennan's arrival in Belfast. As it turned out he stayed much longer than was originally intended, necessitating the detailed letters written by Mrs. M'Tier to his parents from which we get the fascinating picture of his happy, endearing nature, of her remarkably sound ideas about upbringing, and of her loving and devoted care.

---

\* A stopping place on the journey to Belfast

# Chapter II : Two years old

TOM SETTLED INTO his new surroundings immediately, and it was only natural that this novel importation into Belfast society should arouse considerable interest among Mrs. M'Tier's friends and acquaintances. In a few days she writes thus to Dublin: 'Tom's spirits are immoderate. You cd. not know him in Dublin. Yesterday he reigned over a Bowl of two quarts of cockles of which he was so fond that he hoarded the shells to give them a second sucking. It is impossible he can accept half of his invitations, and he is call'd in to so many Houses on his way to his G. Mother's that he seldom reaches it in time. In short you need never hope to make a nursery boy of him again'.[1] Within a couple of weeks of his arrival, and without the slightest hesitation, Matty took him with her on a week-end visit to a country house. One wonders repeatedly, on reading these subsequent letters, how this elderly and, so far as we know, inexperienced matron, with her long flowing skirts, white muslin fichus and large, stiffened caps, coped with the many situations, awkward and otherwise, which must have arisen. But there is never a suggestion of embarrassment or uncertainty. From the beginning the two-year-old accompanied her everywhere without any indication that, in his aunt's view, children should be seen and not heard.

*He is the delight of two familys* [she writes] *and all of my acquaintance are asking for a Day of him, nor can you wonder when I tell you that he has never frown'd & but once cry'd. When I left him at Miss Mateer's he insisted on following me and Miss Betty Mateer brought him in, put him to bed and asleep to a psalm tune. He calls Dr.*

*Mateer 'Papa' with an Arch smile, as if he were making
game of him. The old man is highly amused with him,
particularly when he runs thro' the house calling a little
Dog named Pinch by crying Pish, Pish. He has got several
words already, & many things are so new to him that his
ideas are enlarging every day. I have no doubt that in
three months he will gain more than many young men by
the grand tour. The first object he casts his eye on in the
morning is yr. picture, with which he converses and laughs
for half an hour. He is the most perfectly sweet-tempered
child I ever beheld. My Mother is up and well again. . . .
When she saw Tom go off at eight o'Clock with my Servant & heard he allowed her to put him to bed, she
declared in her life she never saw so sweet a creature.*[1]

Again, on the King's birthday—

*I am just returned with your delighted Son from seeing a
fine regt. troop going thro' their birthday evolutions, &
found a secret pride that he stood his ground firm, tho'
the fire was in his very face, while a Bruce and a Joy fled.*[2]

[These were older children of life-long friends.]
And, in a postscript to Sarah, there is this charming sentence:

*How much of my present happiness I owe to you. 'Tis
long since the eye of joy welcomed my return or beamed
on me with the fond regard my little pet now delights me
by. If I awake before him I contemplate his sweet, sleeping countenance. If he wakes he kisses me awake, & if I
complain of head ach [sic] he forbears & trys by quiet to
go to sleep. What can a two year old do more?*[2]

The very beggars were quick to note the child's unusual
charm, and to exploit it. The letter just quoted contains this
sentence: 'You must allow him pocketmoney, for there are
so many blessing prayed on him that it will break me

rewarding them'.² This chance remark refers to a now out-moded form of public assistance. At that time in Belfast, and elsewhere, the able-bodied, deserving poor of the community were licensed to beg within the confines of the town. Badges were given to these 'sturdy beggers' as a guarantee to the public of their *bona fides*, and to distinguish them from interlopers from outside for whom the town considered it had no responsibility.

In spite of Matty's proud boast that she was 'never a slave to fear' all this joy gave way to instant anxiety when any sign of illness occurred. An outbreak of chincough [whooping-cough] necessitated flight to the country. Cabin Hill was her chosen destination, but a visit there had to be negotiated with tact. So, 'I went over to Miss Young [then living in her town house] & told her I would take a lodging in Holy-wood* for the sake of bathing Tom. She said it was quite foolish, & the pump at C.H. wd. do just as well. This was all I wanted for I did not choose we shd. pin ourselves down on her without her choice.'² So on a sunny June morning, 'he sets off in a chaise with Miss Young and his Aunt to be at C.Hill in time to receive the beds.'³

The country cottage was the beginning of still more enchanting experiences:

*In every place & with every person Tom is happy and makes all about him love him. He gains daily on Miss Y.* [this was very important] *& is her theme to any chance visitors we see. . . . He delights in taking a stranger by the hand, and, being for the first time sent to Town yesterday on a Car to bring out my sister, she says every motion of him was to accommodate her, & be polite* [aged two and a quarter years! ]. *My mother immediately got out of bed*

---

* A village on Belfast Lough.

*& looked out of the window after him as far as she could
see him. We think he is getting fat. I give him half a pint
of warm milk morning and night, he attends the Bier for
it, and rides* [on the farm horse] *before a namesake of his
own, a Hammy from the Cottown,* and he insists on the
gardener wheeling him round the Garden in his barrow.*[4]

We may think that this chivalrous attitude towards guests
was an overstatement on the part of Mrs. M'Tier, but again
and again it will be noted. Far from being shy with strangers
they seem to have called out a most endearing quality in this
happy, friendly child. He was also immensely observant and
a great mimic. On one occasion Miss Bigger, known temporarily to Tom as 'Ann Jane' and later as 'Cousey', was out
of sorts and filled with self-pity. Tom, sensing the situation,
made straight for a bottle of peppermint—'tho', she says,
'he never saw her taste it', and soothingly urged, ' "Ann Jane
take a dop of this," a story that is repeated often with tears
and assertions that "there never was such a child".'[5] On
another occasion Miss Bigger, lying wearily on her couch and
totally unresponsive to Tom's repeated requests of 'Ann Jane
look at 'at', was rudely called to attention by an impatient
scream—'Damn it, look at 'at'.

Instant inquiries revealed that the awful word had been
learned from John the gardener, and Tom 'finding it of
importance' used it with increasing vigour; 'but,' writes his
Aunt, 'I do not think he intends the word, he is smiling all
the time like an Angel & does it to make them laugh'.

Neither in the town house nor in the country is there any
mention of nursery premises, instead we get the picture of a
happy child rambling at will from room to room, delighting
in company. One afternoon at Cabin Hill he found his way
into the kitchen when some horse-play was in progress
between Kitty, a maid, and one of serving-men. Tom, taking

---

* A district in Co. Down where Miss Young owned property,

a serious view of the struggle, burst excitedly into the parlour where the three ladies were enjoying a few moments of
peaceful relaxation, and 'such a story he made out & with
such action of the attack on Kitty & that *he* cried "Kitty be
good, Kitty dear, be good" that we all went into the kitchen
to understand the matter, which [adds Matty philosophi-
cally] I suppose will end in marriage'.[5] Recollecting, however, that all this might sound strange to the anxious mother
in Dublin, she confidently adds this disarming sentence:
'You will exclaim "Does he get leave to stay in the kitchen?"
Ours is not a common one'.

As with all children of his age, most things found their
way into his mouth, though this was strictly forbidden:

*The other day he swallowed a plumb stone and shew'd me*
*what he had done with it. Yesterday he got a bead, & on*
*my looking for it pointed to his throat. I wished to*
*frighten him and instantly took him up and whipt him—*
*'twas but three gentle taps on his bottom—till Miss Bigger*
*cried out against me that she cd. not sit in the room & see*
*that child beat. He, of course, ran to her. 'He has swal-*
*lowed a bead,' said I. 'No,' she replied, 'upon my con-*
*science, there it is in his hand. The child was only joking*
*& you ought not to be so hasty.' 'Then he deserved the*
*correction for the lie,' I replied. 'A very great officer*
*indeed you are,' and the tears as much in her eyes as*
*Tom's.*[6]

In spite of conscious effort, training and discipline in such
circumstances must have been very difficult. 'With six
women,' laments Mrs. M'Tier, 'and two men all devoted to
him 'tis hardly possible he cd. not be taken care of—but as
unlikely he shd. not be *spoiled* . . . and the variety of
amuse't., the great liberty, the pleasure all take in pleasing
him has made him impatient of the least control.' 'And,' she
admits, 'to make him bold I have contributed, I teach him to

jump, to throw stones with the boys, to swing, to go without
shoes and stockings, etc.—how then can I expect him to
remain quiet and out of mischief.' A cold bath [still the spartan training] was part of the dressing routine each morning
'which Tom detested', and finding that direct opposition was
of no avail, took revenge '(though laughingly) by stealing
everything he can get, Bonnets, caps, ribands, etc. etc. & putting them into the Cistern through the Day. This, not being
always conv't., has been remonstrated against & the other
day punished slightly—which he resented *very highly* to
Miss B. and me, colored like scarlet, put his hands behind
his back, walk'd out of the room, & when at a conv't. distance, looked back and call'd us bold jades.'[7] One can only
infer from this that the language in the 'uncommon' kitchen
was not always above reproach!

In spite of Tom's protest Dr. Drennan was anxious that
the daily cold bath should be continued, though he admits
that 'the trials made of it here seemed to disagree with him,
and Wm. [the next child] does not seem to agree with it
much better. I don't suppose you could get him to drink a
little Salt Water mixed with fresh, a tea-cup full every
second morning might be of service. His bowels are weak
and easily distended which gives him rather a large Belly
and may produce worms, which are seldom of much injury.'[8]

Not content with introducing Tom to the joys of the
country, Mrs. M'Tier set off with him one day to Holy-
wood, the little watering-place on Belfast Lough, so that he
might 'see the Sea. He stood at the very edge of it & was
greatly delighted with several Boats, &, like other great men,
in throwing stones into it. I mean to spend a day with him
there next week.'[9]

But Belfast had its own particular delights, and during a
short visit to the house in town—there was constant coming
and going between Cabin Hill and the Parade—Tom spent

PLATE II: DR. WILLIAM DRENNAN.

*This portrait by Robert Home is unfinished, the
likeness being considered so excellent the artist was
not allowed to proceed further.*

much of his time with the pavors, who were engaged in laying the roadway in front of his grandmother's house, 'his
hammer working, till at night he *asks* to go to bed'. The
soldiers on sentry duty were another source of interest. 'On
Sunday,' writes Matty,

> *I went to Meeting & finding him in his wonted station in*
> *the Sentry Box* [the two-year-old], *I sent him home. He*
> *went, and told them he wanted his hat, to go with his*
> *Aunt. He got it and proceed'd, right after me to Arthur*
> *St. but instead of turning proceeded to the far end, where*
> *finding another Box, and an acquaintance in it, he steped*
> *in & staid long enough to create a great alarm—two*
> *messengers, Nancy in an agony, etc. etc. 'till the Soldier*
> *nearest, knowing his taste, pointed him out.*[10]

And again:

> *Were you to come to the Parade now you wd. likely find*
> *yr. Son on guard, as he spends at least two hours every*
> *day in & about the Sentry Box with his own gun, and*
> *tells the soldiers he is going to shoot Bonaparte. . . . The*
> *soldiers are very fond of him, & I leave him under their*
> *care wishing much to make him manly and fearless. How*
> *he will relish Dublin after this sort of life I do not know.*

For the militant toddler of those days Boneparte and the
French took the place of Hitler and the Germans, and toy
guns were as popular then as now. 'Boneparte is his constant
theme, he is perpetually shooting and talking of him.'

The agreed three months had already passed, and letters
from Dublin contain suggestions about Tom's return, a
thought that was as a thrust of cold steel in the heart of Mrs.
M'Tier, though she valiantly endeavoured to see things
from the point of view of his parents. 'I repeat,' she writes to
her sister-in-law, 'that I should be glad Tom wd. remain
with me this winter, but that I shall resign him as cheerfully

as I can whenever you desire it.' 'I do all in my power to prevent him forgetting any of you, & as he is fond of storeys, introduce you in them, and he says he will tell you the one of the Babes in the Wood.' Then came the news of the death of the little daughter whose pending birth had been one of the arguments in favour of Tom's visit. On hearing this sad report Matty's first reaction was anxiety for Tom. She flew upstairs to the child who was sleeping peacefully, 'and, thinking he looked like her, I for the first time loved him with *fear*, determined tomorrow to get him new flannel coats, tho' but an hour before I thought their shortness, even thro' the winter wd. make him hardy. Had I heard the late event sooner I wd. have been more sparing of what I believed did him good . . . the Pums, as he calls them. It is amazing how he prattles with a voice that touches everyone who has either heart or Ear, and in every movement he is genteel.'[13] Matty knew quite well how his mother's heart must now yearn for her first-born—'It is surely natural that you shd. wish for Tom, formed as he is to chase away melancholy, to give future promise, and in the new character of a sweet prattler delight his fond Parents. . . . What a balm he wd. be to you.'[14]

But, against all that there was the marked improvement in his health—how could he stand the pent-up conditions in the city?—and her own despair at the thought of losing him. So the arguments go on in the correspondence, until one day, old Mrs. Drennan, opening a letter of Matty's directed to Dublin added, unobserved, this blotted, 'tremulous line, "I won't part with Tom while I live",'[15] and somehow it was decided that he should stay in Belfast. Many times in this story one imagines that, in spite of a loving husband and still more babies, Sarah must often have longed for her sweet Thomas.

Meantime, the foundations of education were being laid. Mrs. M'Tier suggested that his parents would send, by a friend travelling to Belfast, 'some memorial to my darling, a book of pictures wd. be most acceptable, for he has gone thro' the *Antiquities of Greece*. He knows all his letters and most of the Birds and beasts in a book of them sent from the Miss Buntins.' But the illustrated copy of *Aesop's Fables* that eventually arrived called forth nothing but scorn.

> *Orr will tell you* [Matty writes to Sarah] *how Tom received his present. He has generally a word for the Day & 'I declare' was the one then. To say the truth* neither *of you appears to me so knowing in the reading education as I am myself. Your* pictures *are highly valued—but as for the reading—Old Aesop may suit yr. Doctor's taste, but will never bring on my Boy, or any other, in reading. When I kept my little school* [she continues] *there was a book that delighted children & that they cd. read just after learning their letters. It began 'There was a little boy—a very little boy, for if he had been a big boy etc. etc.' This is the language a child can understand, the words he can spell & the story which amuses & thus instructs . . . A 2d. sheet of letters has done perfectly well for Tom. Playthings he does not want, as an inducement to exercise & amusing himself alone he has a gun, a car & a kite. If you meet* true infantine *little Books send me some.*[16]

In self defence Dr. Drennan replied that *Aesop's Fables* had been sent 'merely for the sake of the *pictures*' but without doubt it was Mrs. M'Tier who knew how to delight a child. Repeatedly she mentions reading aloud and story-telling: 'in none does he take so much pleasure as that about his Papa, when a little boy, going into a field,' being thrown from a horse, having his arm broken and lying in bed a long, long time, 'this is a tale he often asks for'.[17]

In spite of her admonitions Dr. Drennan continued with his strangely formal ideas for Tom's education. Just before the child's third birthday he wrote:

*I hope you are beginning to exercise his head as well as his Feet. Have you try'd his memory? Has he gotten any-thing by heart, as they call it? It will teach him to pro-nounce* correctly *and by imitating feeling he will learn to feel, and to speak interestingly, I don't doubt but you could make him understand the story that gave occasion to the following Lines of Cowper, which I remembered on a third reading, and in a little time he might repeat them as a dole-ful Ditty.*[18]

The 'following lines' for the child to 'get by heart' were stanzas from *The Loss of the Royal George*!

Matty's reply, on this difference of principle, was con-tained in a long epistle to Sarah; writing of Tom she says:

*His letters big & small are quite familiar to him, he begins to know their sound & can spell two columns before three years old. This I fear is not remarkable enough either to please his Father, or to be inserted in his Life, but I cannot torture his memory, which is sufficiently good for the moment, by rigmarole verses, nor a company by setting him up to recite them, neither they nor he understanding them. Nor do I understand what Wm. means by repeating to learn* feeling: *the only one cd. be excited in Tom by The Loss of the R. George wd. be* terror *of a ship. My great aim at present is to* keep *him frank & fearless, and lay the foundations of a manly independence. He fears to look at neither man nor woman, nor to address them without being directed. As for* manners, *he has never been taught any by me, yet never gives offence, but always contrives to attract and please. He picks up vulgar words & well remembers to change them when he wishes to please . . . . I have just been teach-ing him to blow his nose & hold his handkerchief & he has got that* by heart, *& let me tell you it is what some*

*are very disagreeable in. . . . I hope to keep Tom free of
all dirty tricks for they are apt to stick.*[19]

The letter continues with a long account of one of Tom's
conquests, which, for its sure touch, must be given in full:

*Your boy has become a theme for the power of pleasing.
Mrs. T. Sinclaire* [wife of a foremost linen bleacher] *. . .
insisted on his spending a day with her. I left him there
at 11, sent for him at 3, but his stay for Dinner was
requested. I sent at 6, but they begged he might stay for
tea, at eight I sent two woman, one with a Lantern & the
other to carry him, but Mr. Sinclaire brought him home in
his arms. . . . I find he gave full scope to all his little
powers in every way he thought wd. amuse. He danced,
he acted Sir John Falstaff calling, 'Boy, bring me a cup
of sack'* [still not three years old] *& told all his storys
without ever being asked. One he is now particularly fond
of, founded on fact, he repeats with such glee as to excite
great laughter—I shall try to give it to you in his own
words: People thought Thomas was lost, and so they
looked everyplace but could not find Thomas. So!—they
went to John Anderson's* [the gardener] *but Thomas
was not there and to the garden, but he was not there, and
Cousey was very angry. So!—Thomas had gone in to his
own room & shut the door & sat down on the pot, with
his little stool before him & all his books on it, and his
Aunt Atier's bed gown about his shoulders. And he was
taken to Cousey's room—so!—she was very angry and
said 'You little Dog, you were doing nothing there.'
'Fate,' said Thomas, 'I was puffing,' the wit of which
tickles his imagination so much that he always laughs
heartily at the right place—at the end of the story. It is
really curious that a child of his age shd. go into a House
of strangers, without children and remain there as long as
they chose. It is that charming frankness & love of recom-*

*mending himself, with never ceasing good humour—*
*laughing going to bed & smiling coming out of it—which*
*renders him particularly attractive.*[20]

Here, again, is this natural interest in strangers and, as
Matty put it, 'the power of pleasing'.

As with every imaginative child the boundary between
truth and falsehood was ill-defined. His worried Aunt
exclaims: 'He tells lies perpetually & *even upon his honour*,
for he understands *fun* better than truth'.[21] 'What shall I do
or how shall I teach him *truth*, there is no believing a word
he says. I wd. rather he was hanged than a liar.' Again—'I
hope he will soon know what truth is; I hoped it was natural,
except in self defence, but realy it is not so with him & till
I can make him understand it, perhaps it is best not to notice
such slips from it.'[22] How wise she was: but to illustrate her
difficulty she relates the following incident to Sarah:

*I shall give you his history this morning. At 7 he assured*
*me he cd. not sleep any longer for a pain in his back.*
*When dress'd he went to the Kitchen where our female*
*Servts. breakfast early. He ate bread & Butter & cream,*
*sugar & water. He then went into the parlor & studied*
*the Arms, Spears etc. used by the Greeks—at 9 he joined*
*the man in Buttermilk Porridge—after that he shared my*
*toast & when Miss Bigger's breakfast commenced, he*
*modestly declined any more, preferring carrying in Turf.*
*This kept him till Miss B. brought him to me saying, 'I*
*wish you wd. pay some attention to this child—there he*
*is all scratched with gravel. He fell in the Avenue & I*
*found him there without a soul with him'. I asked Tom*
*some question, which he wd. not answer, but said he wd.*
*tell all to Cousey. To her he went & in words & violent*
*gesture informed her that a big, mad Bull had beat Tom,*
*that no one came to him, tho' he cried and broke at the*
*bones. . . . He went on with his story with fresh additions*

*each time* [obviously based on the favourite tale about his father mentioned earlier in this chapter] ... *After this detail & Turf-cadging till* 1 *o'Clock, he insisted on a plate of champ, otherwise parsnips & potatoes, a round hole & a piece of butter. With a Plough-boy's share of this he went to bed & is now fast asleep.*[22]

In the late autumn of this year Dr. Drennan made a short visit to Belfast and sends his wife this charming picture of his re-union with Tom. He and his sister Nancy drove out to Cabin Hill in a chaise and, arriving at the gate,

*decry'd my sister M'Tier in the avenue, and when she saw us, running back to the Hall-Door, where with our First-born in her hand, which he quitted only to clap his hands above his head in expectation of seeing us. Dear Sarah, he looked delightfully, in ruddy health and his countenance sparkling with good spirits and good humour. I never felt myself a Father so much as at this happy moment, no, not when he first came to my arms. He did not, I am sure, know me perfectly* [at first] *but on my knee he was in an instant as familiar, and* talkative *as ever you could have wished. Sweet is his voice, in his manner lively to a degree, and yet as gently as possible. I was indeed impressed on seeing him look so engagingly at first sight. I was proud of him. Ah, dear Sarah you would have been at that time a happy Mother had you seen him with me. He has never once cry'd, as they assure me, since he came to this place, and, notwithstanding the credulity of a Father, I am inclined to believe it is the real fact from the habit of good humour which his Features appear dressed in. He speaks whole sentences, knows all his letters* [he had not been able to talk before leaving Dublin], *tells the names of all the birds & beasts in his little Books, and accompanies everything he says with natural and animated action. He slept with me last night*

*in my sister's bed. .... All rave of our dear Thomas with
whom my letter begins and must end, but don't read it
to anyone. Affection is a sacred thing, but to those not
interested, as we are, it seems a silly thing.*[23]

It seems almost sacrilege to print it now!

This happy visit definitely fixed the idea of his father on
Tom's mind. In the following weeks he was heard to 'quote'
many of the phrases he heard his Papa use. For example:
'Well, well, Kitty,' he declared, 'I will come back just now
and murder you *out of hand.*' Also: 'of himself entirely'
he informed the household 'that his Papa desired he might
be call'd Thomas, not Tom, & even went to the Gard'ner
with the same orders'. Furthermore, 'everything he does not
chuse, he says Papa wont allow it, & I am plagued night &
morning with a new fashioned way of using a certain utensil,
which he assures me was his Papa's method'.[24]

One can well imagine the tussles over 'the certain utensil'
for, with all his exuberant charm, Tom, at two years old,
had a very determined will. 'In the fields the other Day I
recommended his keeping the path way,' writes Mrs.
M'Tier, 'and gave him more reasons than one for it, but in
vain, he told me he would have a path *of his own*'.[25]

But educational progress and social aplomb counted for
nothing compared with Tom's health. There was the normal
procedure of teething. Mrs. M'Tier 'feared he was grown
fretful, thin and pettish, but on finding he had got 4 double
teeth without any worse appearance, I hoped I had discovered the cause'. And, a week or two later, 'I am told by
the attentive girl who watches him that he is getting two
more double teeth—and I have therefore quit bathing for
the present'.[26] This was probably 'going into the bucket' of
cold water. There was also the constant fear of a cough and,
in days when Syrup of Figs and other patent medicines were
as yet unknown, recurring concern about 'the costive state of

his bowels'. For the latter he was 'plied' with fruit—when
he was in town basketfuls of whatever was in season being
delivered from Cabin Hill. For the cough Dr. Drennan
prescribed as follows:

*It might be well to make a waistcoat of thin Welch Flan-
nel, to put next Thomas' skin during the day only, and if his
feet and body be warm I think a little exercise every day
in the open air, either in a carriage or on a car would be
of use. A Burgundy Pitch plaster between the shoulders
might excite a little redness & itching and relieve the
cough, for the worst supposition I can make is that his
tendency to eruption on the surface may have irritated his
lungs. Is his skin quite clear at present? Rhubarb always
griped him much, & once when an infant and Betty had
taken him out after a dose of it, we thought he would have
died with the colic which was removed by a warm bath, etc.
I think whey (renet whey) sweetened with Manna would
be a good drink—and if his skin be dry and hot a few
drops (8 or 9) of antimonial Wine in the whey at bed-
time. Some powders of œthiops mineral (about 10 grains
in each) taken every morning for a fortnight might be of
service to sweeten (as it is called) his blood & is easily
taken in a little treacle. But I am still of opinion that
whenever the cough & feverishness abate, the Bark infusion or decoction, exercise in open air, and jaunting from
country to town frequently would be the best plan, or if
you think his feverishness intermits, and is, in some part
of the day gone, at that time a Wine glass of the cold
infusion of bark might be of service. I know not what
more to say about our Boy.*[27]

Then there is this from Mrs. M'Tier:

*Before I went to bed the other night he was very uneasy
& even wept (I cannot name crying to him). I took him*

*up and sat with him some time on my knee at the fire—*
*the tears often came down & with them he still said 'be*
good, *be good'. He had a restless night & told me he had*
*a sore ear, which, in the morning, I examined, but cd.*
*see nothing in it. He was well all that day, but the next,*
*I found by his cap & the Bolster, his Ear had beeled in*
*the* inside, *slightly, no doubt, but there is not a* woman *in*
*this house that wd. not have mourn'd & prosed over the*
*same for Days. I put a bit of clean cloth on it to keep him*
*from cold—& it does not moisten, nor have I allowed*
*him to go out, for I wd. lament ever seeing him deaf.*[28]

To which Dr. Drennan replied:

*I should not like him to have repeated inflammation in*
*the ear, particularly in the inside. You do not think that*
*it had any connexion with that heaviness and sleepiness he*
*complained of. . . . At any rate, if that should return, or*
*any sign of soreness in the ear by a restless night, I should*
*think some pleasant laxative easily taken, would be useful*
*in the following way—such as Imperial, made by dissolv-*
*ing two tea spoonfulls of cream of tartar in a quart of*
*boiling water with a little lemon-peel, and sweetening it*
*with white sugar to his taste. A half pint of this taken luke*
*warm during the day will affect his bowels, and ought to*
*be taken once every ten days, or whenever he appears*
*heavy, or sleepy in the day time. If his ear should be*
*attacked with great pain, put a warm poultice to it at bed-*
*time, & that will make it the sooner break. The poultice*
*may be made of bread & milk with oil, or a well-boiled*
*onion.*[29]

But already Mrs. M'Tier was writing reassuringly that
'Tom's ear is quite well. . . . He is now standing with a
spoon stealing Pedlar's cream off the top of the Churn, &
in great delight with his success'.[30]

Indeed the year closes on a stirring, active child. 'As a proof of his strength he can lie from 9 'till 9 without rising, or saying more than once "Aunt M'dear turn and kiss me",' and, better still, he runs 'like a *Man*, not like a girl shaking her arms, but erect & straight, both in back & head, & his belly is now so flat I am obliged to *take in* his waistbands, while I lengthen his petticoats. . . . His feats in this house of late have not been strictly decorous; in Miss Young's room he has broke a strong chair and the looking glass, endeared by time more than value. She bore it without reproach, she does not fear the broken glass Omen. Indeed I have longed for the weather allowing Tom to get out after dinner [this was written in February], in order to save the Arm chairs, *over* which he *will* climb, & also his own bones which will be much safer in the fields.'[31] Miss Young bore a good deal 'without reproach'. Her peaceful life at Cabin Hill had been entirely disarranged by this stirring youngster, yet she gave Mrs. M'Tier '5 guineas & a half to purchase two 16ths for him in the Lottery, as she thought different numbers gave the best chance & I made him take up the two he chose, which are 13,044 - 2,067. Thus his father & you [to Sarah] may count figures in the papers every morning for a Month, and Tom mount the pony he is to buy with his prize'.[32]

Even his dear 'Cousey' was the victim of indoor repression 'for in throwing he has twice hit her two remaining teeth, saying "that was a *comely* throw". Where he gets these kind of words I know not, but he is never *far* from their true meaning.'[33]

But everything was forgiven by his adoring Aunt: 'He is grown bold [fearless] for which I believe I am to blame, being rather pleased to hear the freedom of his bolder notes, once like the soft young red-breast, now the louder, strong, joyous flings of the Thrush—music in both. I wonder if every child's voice sounds as sweet in the Parents' ear as Tom's in mine—I fancy not—for there is that in his that

attracts *everyone* & it is curious that everyone thinks he
sounds *their name* sweeter than any other. He is in perfect
health but exercises so much that in the winter afternoons he
always fell asleep or grew cross. I therefore took the old
method of putting him to bed in the forenoon when he takes
a nap of three *hours*, & is, as he says, " 'greeable all day".[34]

Christmas is accorded little mention in Mrs. M'Tier's
chronicle of events, it reminded her too forcibly of earlier,
gayer days. 'This is a dull and different Christmas from what
I once pass'd here, at my time of life there can seldom be
any other,' she wrote in this first year of Thomas's sojourn;
but she adds, 'Tom is a sweet, endearing Hope, for which I
am grateful to Heaven and you. . . . He is well, & going
from room to Room this morning, with his kiss & *seasonable*
wishes—in high spirits.'[35] The presence of this darling child
was already doing much to mitigate her loneliness.

Did Sarah at times wonder if her generous, impulsive
sister-in-law had completely appropriated Thomas? Little
William was now a sturdy toddler, and already the fourth
baby was on its way.

Perhaps when Mrs. M'Tier gave herself time to think
she too wondered if her devotion to Tom was, in fact, usurp-
ing his parents' place, and in self-vindication she passed on
this remark from her friend Miss Greg: 'she thinks you
were but *just* in giving him to me, as she thinks I had a
great share in getting him; and what, she says, so well worth
the trouble, in which I join her'.[36]

# Chapter III: Three years old

THERE is no mention of any celebration for Thomas' third birthday, indeed, one gets the impression from these letters that birthdays did not receive much attention. For Easter Monday, on the other hand—which followed almost immediately—Mrs. M'Tier had planned exciting surprises. It was a 'delightful day' as regards the weather, and Tom set off, full of glee and importance, for a race meeting, 'mounted on the firm arm of his friend Hammy [the yard man], so tall as to give him a full view, & on whose care I could depend. He was on the course from 1 till 4, returned safe & in good spirits . . . & they both sat down, *tête à tête*, to a cold bone and potatoes'. Following on that exciting experience 'a groupe of girls and boys had assembled on my summons, and impatiently forbore to throw their Eggs till Tom arrived. They were afterwards formed into a company of Volrs.* &, with Drum, Sword, Gun, Carr & *Raisins*, were a happy groupe. I really wished [Mrs. M'Tier adds] to have Tom introduced to some innocent boyish sports.' Constantly she was devising schemes that would involve masculine society to counteract the undiluted femininity of Cabin Hill.

It was at this time that Tom was 'introduced' to a dancing class. He and his Aunt, on one of their visiting jaunts, were staying the night with some friends where the dancing master was due to attend the following morning,

*and* [she writes] *I wanted to see what effect that scene wd. have on him—Ladies and Misses all sitting in form. When the man took out his fiddle Tom comes forward,*

---

* Volunteers

*tucking his petticoats tight behind like the girls, cries to*
*Mr. Dumont* [the master], *'Begin,' &, in spite of a uni-*
*versal loud laugh, figured through the room in every*
*direction till, his heart beating, he flew to my lap for*
*approbation.*[1]

Not even the sight of the little girls actually at their lesson
could 'damp his future attempts,' for, on Dumont asking
him 'if he wd. be taught, he answered, "Yes, me will",' and,
taking the master's hand, 'made a curtesy as low as he had
seen. Yet this Boy, on seeing two gentlemen dispute about
a pr. of snuffers & who wd. use them, the night before, burst
out in a loud fit of crying, saying he did not love bloody
noses. Indeed his *courage* does *not* improve, and a boxing
match he saw on the Stage has rendered a play House his
aversion'.[1] Already Mrs. M'Tier was anxious to share with
him her passion for the theatre, and happily the 'aversion'
soon wore off.

While there may have been no celebrations for his birthday, Thomas was now definitely regarded as having left the
toddler stage, and ready for promotion in, among other
things, the matter of clothes. 'I have made him trousers,
body'd as you describe,' Matty wrote to his mother, 'with
which he was much delighted, but had forethought enough
to go to a new man-servant, rather more boyish than our
last, & say, "but how in all the world James do you do with
yr. breeches when you go to puff".'[2]

Evidently this new status, as with all promotion, had its
alarming moments, but the difficulty was successfully negotiated, and in a week or so Matty writes, 'He has got on his
trousers which are quite easy to him. He is every inch a
gentleman's child & so much admired that if it was not for
superior motives, vanity wd. tempt me to keep him in Town,
and put him to dancing, etc'.[3]

Dr. Drennan, for his part, continued to think in terms of
education, expressing his views in this first letter written to

his little son, a long Chesterfieldian epistle which must be
quoted in full, for it provides an essential part of the whole
picture of the child's background:

*My dear little Boy Thomas* [it begins],
    *Your Papa sends you a present of some little books,** 
*that are very pretty, and very good books, and you must
not tear them, or throw them about the room, but keep
them clean, and put them on the shelf in the parlour when
you have done with them. And your Papa hopes that you
will soon be able to read them all, and to tell pretty stories
out of them to your Aunt, and Cousins, and then you will
laugh and be very happy. And your Papa is in Dublin, a
great way off, a great deal further off than Belfast, where
grandmama and Aunt Anne live, but Papa remembers his
little Thomas, and he sends this Letter to little Thomas
to tell him that he loves him, and that, if he be a good
Boy, he will soon be able to write himself to his Papa, but
before he can write, he must first learn to read, and Papa
sends him these little Books to teach him to read.*
    *And Uncle Edward† will give these little Books to
Thomas from his Papa, and little Thomas must thank
Uncle Edward for being so good as to carry these books
all the way from Dublin to little Thomas; for Uncle
Edward is a very good young Man and was very fond of
little Thomas and Thomas ought to be fond of him, and
walk with him, and show him the garden and all his play
things.*
    *And Mama sends her Love to her dear little Thomas—
Don't you remember Mama, pretty Mama and good
Mama, that was so fond of Thomas when he was a good*

---

* by Mrs. Barbauld

† a brother of Sarah's in Dublin on business.

*Boy, and liv'd in Dublin, where there are plenty of goose-*
*berries and strawberries and apples in the shops, and when*
*Thomas comes to Dublin to Papa & Mama, Mama will*
*buy fruit for Thomas every day, if he learns to read, and*
*is a good Boy, and never cries. And there is a pretty*
*garden in Dublin where little Thomas may dig with a*
*spade, and there is a hobby horse with a fine mane and*
*tail, for Thomas to ride on.*

*But Thomas must be a very good Boy while he stays at*
*Cabin-Hill and remember all that his Aunt and his*
*Cousin, and Anne Jane say to him; and say his prayers*
*every night, and kneel down, and say 'God bless me and*
*keep me a good Boy, and make me live to be an Honest*
*Man, and bless Papa, and Mama and Grand-Mama and*
*Aunt 'Tier and Aunt Anne, and Couzn. Young who is so*
*good to me, and Cozn. Anne Jane, and all the People in*
*this House'.*

*And Papa writes this letter to Thomas, and bids him*
*never to go upon the road by himself, and that he may*
*laugh heartily but never to cry, and to go to bed when he*
*is bid, and never to puff in company, but if he wants to*
*puff to go out of the room and to stay at the Hall-Door*
*untill he counts five upon his Fingers.*

*And Thomas has a little brother in Dublin and they*
*call him William, and he has been very ill, and because*
*he was ill and had a pain in his breast he was very cross,*
*but he is now better and growing a good boy, like*
*Thomas; and Thomas is bigger than his brother William*
*and older, a whole year older, and a year is a long time,*
*a great many days. And when Thomas comes to Dublin he*
*will play with his brother William and be good to him,*
*and show him all his playthings.*

*And Betty who was a Nurse to Thomas, sends her love*
*to him, for she loves him dearly, and so does James the*
*manservant. And Papa and Mama desire Thomas to give*

PLATE III: MRS. MARTHA M<sup>c</sup>TIER.

*Aunt m'dear.*

*their Love to Aunt 'Tier and to good Cozen Young and Coz. Biggar, and to tell Grand-mama, when he goes to Belfast, that Thomas has got a letter from Papa that is, his Father. And let Thomas keep this Letter, because it is the first he ever got, and because it comes from Papa, and because Papa's Father would have wrote such a Letter to Papa when he was a little Boy, like Thomas. And so sweet Thomas and pretty Thomas, and what is better than both, good little Thomas, Farewell—and remember Papa loves you, and will teach you to write Letters to Aunt 'Tier when you come to Dublin.*

*William Drennan.*[4]

*Dublin,*
*Marlborough Street, 33,*
*June 13, 1804.*

On wonders if Dr. Drennan, recalling his sister's sample [p. 19] of the kind of story a child enjoyed, had tried hard to draft this letter accordingly. In other circumstances he could write with unusual tenderness and sympathy, but—like many fathers—he was quite unable, when he made the conscious effort, to get to the level of his own little son. How much more genuine is this spontaneous message: 'Remember me to Thomas and tell him I longed to take a walk with him on the shore and pick pretty shells near the Rock'.[5] One hopes that, for Thomas, the novelty of receiving a letter made up for the formality of its contents.

Children's books are mentioned frequently in this correspondence, and it is well to remember that they were at this period a comparatively novel development. For untold generations children had been entertained by fairy stories, fables, rhymes and time-honoured tales passed on, for the most part, by oral tradition, though, with the increase of printing, some of them were set out in chapbooks and broadsheets. 1719 and 1726 had seen the publication, respectively, of *Robinson*

*Crusoe* and *Gulliver's Travels,* books not written specifically
for children. As early as 1715 Isaac Watts had published his
*Divine and Moral Songs.* These may be described as a hang-
over from Puritan days, their purpose being 'to quicken and
revive the dying devotion of the age', but they continued to
form an impressive part of any child's repertoire for many a
decade to come, and Thomas would know all about the
following:

> Let Dogs delight to bark and bite
>     For God has made them so;
> Let Bears and Lions growl and fight,
>     For 'tis their Nature too.

And this about the Bees:

> How skillfully she builds her cell:
>     How neat she spreads the wax,
> And labours hard to store it well
>     With the sweet food she makes.

> In works of labour or of skill
>     I would be busy too;
> For Satan finds some mischief still
>     For idle hands to do.

By the close of the century, however, the ideas of Rousseau
and the Age of Reason were well launched, and, in order to
provide a new and superior standard of education and entertainment, a great advance was made in the writing and
publication of attractive books specially prepared for
children.

In 1764 the *London Chronicle* carried an advertisement
from John Newbery—later to become famous in this particular line of business:

> *Mr. Newbery intends to publish the following important
> volumes, bound and gilt, and hereby invites all his little
> friends who are good to call for them at the Bible and*

Sun, *in* St. Paul's Churchyard: *but those who are naughty are to have none.*

The list of titles includes *The Renowned History of Giles Gingerbread*; *The Valentine Gift: or How to behave with honour, integrity and humanity*: *very useful with a Trading Nation*; and *The Fairing, or Golden Present for Children*. 'And,' added Mr. Newbery, 'there is in the Press, and speedily will be published . . . *The History of Little Goody Two Shoes.*' *The Lilliputian Magazine* followed soon afterwards. Goldsmith called Newbery 'the philanthropic publisher of St. Paul's Churchyard'. The little books were sold at sixpence each.

Then, in 1780, the majestic figure of Mrs. Barbauld burst upon the scene, with her *Lessons for Children*, written, in the first instance, for her two-year-old nephew Charles, the child who lived with the Barbaulds as their own son. In the following year she published *Hymns in Prose*. Mrs. Barbauld had a school for little children and both books were written from her practical experience of what could be easily comprehended, and with a strongly emphasised didactic and moral purpose.

Mrs. Barbauld has been extolled for her masterly command of the English language, an accomplishment which she adapted, but never abandoned, in her writing for children. She was a member of the Aikin family, the noted dissenters of Warrington, whose social background and intellectual outlook accorded so closely with that of the Drennans, and it is easy to understand this note of appreciation from Dr. Drennan: 'I am glad you like Mrs. Barbauld's little volumes. I think all her writings excellent and I believe her very sincerely religious'.[6]

Mrs. Trimmer and Miss Edgeworth are next in succession, with others of less consequence, indeed between 1790 and 1820 there were at least a dozen successful writrs for children including Thomas Day of *Sandford and Merton* fame.

Many of these books were beautifully produced with delightful woodcuts and engravings. The high moral tone and
serious purpose continued, and increased, until Charles
Lamb, in a fury of indignation, wrote to Coleridge in 1802:

> *Goody Two Shoes is almost out of print. Mrs. Barbauld's
> stuff has banished all the old classics of the nursery, and
> the shop-man at Newbery's hardly deigned to reach them
> off an old exploded corner of a shelf, when Mary asked
> for them. Mrs. Barbauld's and Mrs. Trimmer's nonsense
> lay in piles about. Knowledge, insignificant and vapid as
> Mrs. Barbauld's books convey, it seems must come to a
> child in the shape of knowledge; and his empty noodle
> must be turned with conceit of his own powers when he
> has learnt that a horse is an animal, and Billy is better
> than a horse, and such like, instead of that beautiful
> interest in wild tales, which made the child a man, while
> all the time he suspected himself to be no bigger than a
> child. Science has succeeded to poetry no less in the little
> walks of children than with men.* [An observation that
> could be made with relevance today.] *Is there no possi-
> bility of averting this sore evil? Think* [he demands of
> Coleridge] *what you would have been now, if instead of
> being fed with tales and old wives' fables in childhood,
> you had been crammed with geography and natural
> history.*
> *Hang them!* — *I mean the cursed Barbauld crew, those
> blights and blasts of all that is human in man and child.*[7]

One imagines that Dr. Drennan would have stoutly
defended Mrs. Barbauld, he himself could be so ponderously
improving when he thought the occasion demanded it:
Matty, on the other hand, would have been more sympathetic with Charles and Mary Lamb. There is no mention in
her letters that *Tales from Shakespeare*, published in 1807,
ever reached her, but we can imagine—great story-teller and

play-lover that she was—how she would have hailed it with delight. At any rate when she scorned *Aesop's Fables* and demanded some 'true infantine little books' [see p. 19] Mrs. M'Tier knew exactly what she wanted.

But to get back to Thomas. It seems that he sent a present to his parents in return for the little books, and certainly his Aunt's communication to Dublin is missing in which she commented with some asperity on the parental letter, for, in a few days, Dr. Drennan writes: 'We are both much indebted to Thomas for his present which is a very solid answer to my Letter, but as neither he nor his Aunt seem to think much of my composition in that line, I shall not trouble him with so many epistles as I designed to do'. Nevertheless, within a short space of time, he was sending to his sister a hymn, nine verses long, composed by himself, with this instruction: 'Make Tom (if he has any memory) try to get the following Hymn by heart'. Here are the first and last verses:

> O Sweeter than the sweetest Flower,
>     At Evening's dewy close,
> The Will, united with the Pow'r
>     To succour human woes.

> 'Tis he who scatters blessings round,
>     Adores his Maker best:
> For him whose life was mercy-crown'd
>     The Bed of Death is bless'd.[8]

The next letter from Belfast ended with this laconic postscript: 'Yr. verses are good—so is Tom's memory, surely these will not impress a 3 yrs. old'.[8]

Cowper's *John Gilpin* was quite another matter. One day he and his Aunt were taken by 'jaunting Carr' to Mount Pottinger, the scene of the dancing class mentioned earlier. Their driver, Mr. Ferguson, was perched aloft on the 'chair

seat', a high wind blowing his coat in billows at either side.
Quick as lightning Tom remarked that 'he was just like John
Gilpin—to the high entertainment of the party', Mrs.
M'Tier explaining to her brother that he had laughed
heartily when she had read the poem to him some days
before, and now *'intirely of himself did apply it as I said'*.[10]

No! Matty's idea of education was quite different. During
one of Tom's sojourns in Belfast she had taken him 'to see
paper & bricks made & I think he will not forget it'[11]—
enchanting for a precocious child who enjoyed the infor-
malities of education rather than its formalities. Much of his
time was spent with the neighbours, especially his favourite
Dr. Mateer. 'He is just arrived from Dr. Mateer's in high
lift of Spirits & dirt, having fallen into the guttars'.[11] On
another occasion he was reported to be in fits of laughter at
Dr. Mateer 'scourging a top'. The old gentleman adored the
child, and they were the best of companions. 'But,' writes his
Aunt, 'I believe I will send him to C: Hill to range the
fields, bring in the turf and duck in cold water.'[11] While
ordinary lessons were boring 'the *Tea-Kettle Family* was
Tom's delight for a day—pictures he never tires of—but
studys them repeatedly. He wd. come on well in reading ( I
mean knowing some little words) if he cd. keep awake—but
the truth is he hates it & his papa's presents must turn to
benefit in his *own hands*.'[12] Within reason, she would let the
child learn in his own way.

He continued to command the adoration of all. A young
man, spending an evening in the house, crept up to the bed-
room to look at Tom asleep. He told stories to old Mrs.
Drennan's attendant, saying, 'Tell my Grandmother, they
will make her laugh'. 'He feeds her [his grandmother] with
gooseberries, takes the skins from her & bids God Bless her
every night, & asks me to teach him to pray for her.'[13]

Ridicule he could not endure; Tom was far too sensitive
for such a cruel weapon. 'He has taken a total disrelish to

the Sinclaires,* the only reason he will tell us is that one day
Maryanne made faces at him'[14]; and 'Lennox Bigger was
here lately & seeing him cut paper call'd him *Miss* which he
cannot forget, for ridicule he cannot bear & I cd. make him
cry at any time by laughing at him'.[15] An interesting reference, by the way, to the pleasure children always find in
using scissors.

That the servants were completely at his mercy, this
'Tommy-anecdote', as Mrs. M'Tier called such stories,
illustrates:

> *All Winter I have sat at my fire till Tom went to sleep,
> tho' when I chose to leave him he did not object. For
> some nights past he has recommended me to go down to
> my Supper, but leave the Door open. After I had done so
> last night I heard him calling, 'Kitty come & find the
> thing in my Bed, come woman'. I went in & found the
> 'thing' to be a slice of Meal & suet Dumplin fry'd, &
> jumping about as firm as beef. He listens when supper
> goes into the parlor & inveigles by his voice & fun even
> this proper girl, who he keeps in continued fits of laughter
> ... I have no doubt but all Servants indulge children in
> tea particularly, a thing they can never believe will hurt
> anybody, even in the poisonous manner they take it them-
> selves. Tom is very fond of it, but it is little more than
> warm milk tinctured—but he gets a very hearty supper
> & sleeps soundly.*[16]

Unfortunately, the cook at Cabin Hill was not above
exploiting the child for her own ends:

> *There is an old woman as cook here, who is particularly
> disagreeable to Miss Bigger, & who has told Tom that if*

---

* the family of a brother of Thos. Sinclaire (p.21)

*he brings all the pins he gathers she will give him plenty
of cream & butter. This arrangement has been kept
strictly, I believe, on both sides—as Miss Biggers caps &
bonnets testify—and tho' Tom is almost perfection in her
eyes, taking her pins to give to Sally Scott, is what she
cannot brook. Often he has been forbid to put her to this
severe tryal, but in vain, everything flew in streamers that
a pin could fasten. This day I gave him a slap for it & a
prick of a pin. The fire flashed out of his eye and he—
spit—in my face. I turn'd up his bottom & gave him a
tap, when he went off to the Door & looking back said,
'if you dare to take a pin of Sally Scotts I will turn up yr.
petticoats & whip your bottom.' Here the contest ended.[7]*
[Mrs. M'Tier repeatedly showed her good sense by not
carrying an argument too far!]

This is the least pleasant of all the 'Tommy anecdotes', and
the air of unconcerned glee with which Matty relates the
incident in a letter to Sarah may appear rather strange,
especially as it hinged on a grave discourtesy to one of the
old ladies. But there it is; it must all have seemed extremely
amusing at the time!

Thomas still delighted in story-telling, either listening or
as the raconteur, and it is to be feared that he was now
regarded more or less as a professional entertainer within
the family circle.

*You cannot have an idea how he went on one night at Dr.
Mateer's. A few minutes after John Kennedy came into
the room, he mounted on his feet unask'd & said he wd.
tell him a story, which he did thus—'Mr. Scot was dying.
Well! Mrs. Mateer had a little pig,* so it fell into the*

---

* The larger town houses had gardens at the back, and it was usual for
each house to have its pig-sty along with the cow-shed and stables; there would
also be the outside 'privvy'.

*little hole in the House of Commons, & Isaac had to get
a rope & put it round its neck to draw it up. So Miss
Scott came to the window & said O! don't make that
noise, my Brother is dying. Well! the pig cried louder &
louder, for Isaac had to put it in a tub to wash it, & Mrs.
Mateer eat a piece of it to her Dinner, so she did.' You
may guess this raised a good laugh. Soon after, he whis-
pered to me he wanted to go out, & Margt. M'Tier &
Bess Kennedy went with him. They staid so long that
Mrs. Kennedy did more than hint at their ignorance in
the business. Wm. Crombie & Mr. Forbes had come in,
& some time after Tom & the ladies had quietly returned
from their business, Tom calls out loudly, 'Margt. M'Tier
you have not buttoned me right'. This call'd up both the
ladies blushes, which were kept up by the laugh of the
men. I took him home in the chair, when he directly said
'now wasn't I agreeable'.*[18]

The last remark, volunteered in the black darkness of a
sedan chair, conveyed nothing more than a sense of having
fulfilled his normal social obligations to the company. How
on earth he had not become insufferably and permanently
spoiled defies reason, but within a page or two of that letter
we are told that when Miss Young made a pilgrimage into
Belfast to see old Mrs. Drennan and to collect some legal
documents, 'you would have been charmed to see Tom's
delighted attention to her, handing her up & down stairs,
etc. and telling and saying everything he cd. think of to
amuse her, exciting Miss Bigger's observation, "Was there
ever so sweet a creature".' Not even the episode of the 'pins'
could cloud the devotion of the two old ladies, and here
again is an instance of Tom's sensitive awareness of the
whims and requirements of other people—extraordinary in
a child of his age—and his spontaneous, and entirely unself-
conscious, pleasure in satisfying them.

In town and country Tom was now considered old enough to go about, within limits, by himself. 'The situation here [Belfast] is remarkably favourable & I send him to take a turn by *himself* frequently round the Linenhall [*facing p. 64*] in the shrubbery—where horse, Dog, or water cannot enter, and where he will join any *genteel* person who *asks* him.'[19]

One morning Mrs. Leslie, a very 'genteel' neighbour, seeing him pass, called him into her house. The family was still at breakfast and Thomas was offered some bread with butter and jam. He 'declined' the butter, explaining that 'his Aunt did not allow him any as it came up in his mouth very bad'. [No inhibitions about any of nature's reactions!] A little later, and after Thomas had departed, Lord Belfast* bounced in, and finding Mrs. Leslie enjoying some liquorice ball demanded some for himself. This was refused as 'his Mama did not like it' but his young lordship persisted. Whereupon Mrs. Leslie told him the story of another little boy 'who was here just before him. He wd. not believe her, insisted on knowing his name, &, says Tom—who laughs and repeats the story — she said his name was *little Tom Drennan*'.[20]

On one occasion, however, at Cabin Hill, having been left with a supposedly 'safe playfellow', Tom, betraying his Aunt's confidence, went out on the road and later could not be found: to make matters worse Mrs. M'Tier was away for the afternoon. 'The whole house was in an uproar—women and men every different way but the right one. At last he was brought in prisoner, very grave, and Miss Bigger—just swallowing drops—says to him, "You will kill me". "You are not dead yet tho'," said Tom cheekily. "Oh, you will get a whipping when your Aunt returns". This neither made any

---

* Eldest son of 2nd Marquist of Donegall.

impression, for when I came home he says, "I knew you would not whip me for *that*". However, he has promised not to do it again & I can trust to *that*."[21]

This escapade called forth a strong expression of opinion from Dr. Drennan:

*I think you should be on your guard with respect to Tom's playfellow being as safe as you represent him. No doubt it was by his temptation they wandered out of their bounds. I am of my mother's opinion with respect to Servants and children, and you are too credulous with respect to character. People say that Boys teach each other to be manly, but I think it is absurd to let good boys be educated under bad ones, which is always the case, and it is time enough for Tom to be manly ten years hence. I am quite against public schools for children, and what they learn there at the daily risk of their lives; and early habits are formed after the boldest, that is the most mischievous & worst bred boy in the school.... I should much rather leave him by himself, than with his playfellow without watching them, for one will surely lead the other into the ditch. And trust not to his promises, for children will do wrong, not from evil propensity, but merely in pursuit of novelty, untill the habits of doing as they are bid be confirmed.... I am not at all afraid of his getting any formality from old Ladies, or of his being rendered timid; better even so, than boldnes beyond his strength, and that mimicry of manliness which is unnatural in a child. One of these manly children* [he warningly recounts] *tumbled little Fleming, his playfellow, into a common sewer, from which he was rescued with great difficulty, and another manly child run a red-hot iron up his brother's nose when asleep by way of fun. I had much rather see Tom at the good Dr's, whipping the top, than hear of your sending him to play with the*

*Thompsons, Sinclaires, etc. from whom it is an even chance he comes with a bruise or perhaps a broken bone. So much for Thomas at present.*[22]

Such a challenge could not go unanswered, and Mrs. M'Tier began her reply thus:

*I approve of all your observations in regard to children, but there are exceptions to all rules, & Tom shall be manly, without being* wicket. *It is very seldom indeed there is not an eye over him tho' he does not know it, & I take pleasure while I am behind the hedge, to hear him answer questions put by the stranger—tell his name, his Father's, etc. etc. I wish greatly to keep him* very frank, *& fearless, & I send him to walk by himself round the inclosure at the L: Hall, two sides of the square I see. He does not go to play with* any *children & it is Mrs. Sinclaire sends for him.... How are you to educate yr. Boys if not at a public school, for even if you were to be their Master that is a character which does not endear the Father. Kennedy of Cultra dedicated his time to his children, was little better than a schoolmaster, & like most of them was hated.... You have been unfortunate in Servants,\* but when you say you have adopted my Mother's opinions in regard to them & children, I think you are wrong, & hope you will at least fall on a happier mode of treating them. Dishonesty is too common among them, & want of that* exact *truth which is a refined kind of it, neither they, nor most of their betters have an idea of, otherwise, I believe they are just as good as higher ranks. I have known* several *instances of love & kindness (it wd. be termed gratitude perhaps, very improperly) of so disinterested a nature as to deprive themselves of even*

---

\* Betty, the nursemaid, had turned out badly, she and the manservant had been dismissed.

necessarys *to serve a child in a family they have lived
with. Such was one of Mrs. Getty's who spun for lottery
tickets to the boys. Such now feels for the Crombies &
to such Miss Biggar has been often indebted for attendance and kind attentions years after they were from her.
Why then class such in general reprobation? I believe
they are (with just allowances) as good as their
calumniators.*[23]

On this occasion the strength of Mrs. M'Tier's feelings
played havoc with the construction of her sentences—the
strong radical sentiments, which had lain dormant since the
tragedy of '98,* were very easily fanned to a flame.

As for Tom, along side of all the fun and freedom there
was, alas, a good deal of illness during this year. Teething,
and a 'bowel complaint' that lasted for a week, turned the
observant three-year-old into the professional invalid.

*It is curious to see, or rather hear, the change in Tom's
manner of speaking by these few days' petting. He
drawls every word twice as long & talks like an old
woman of sickness, aches & death. Miss Y: asked him
yesterday morning how he was, he answered he had a
poor night, with a bad pain in his loin. She felt this &
seemed so much concerned I was obliged to inform her
that it was but the moment before he had complimented
Miss Biggar by feeling her weak part & assuring her he
got no sleep with a pain in his back. But I'll soon drive
away these fancys or tales & I hope the ladies will see
the folly of such eternal croakings when a very child
repeats them.*[24]

Sometime later, however, there is definite cause for
worry, for Tom's ears are again infected, 'one of them very

---

* Irish Rebellion, 1798

sore, both swelled and several lumps behind them & on his
Neck, call'd wax Kernels, & little pimples'. Dr. Mateer had
seen the child more than once '& makes light of it, not
desiring him to be confined—to be kept open, not much
flesh and to bathe his ears often with Sea water which is
done & I shall add the recept of the *Imperial* Physician'[25]
[*see p. 26*]. The next letter reports one ear still very sore,

> ... & *beeled pimples on his face & neck, which you*
> *know would hurt anyone's looks in a* night *cap; yet his*
> *cheerful, smiling countenance shines thro' all, nor does*
> *medicine cloud it, even in the moment of swallowing.*
> *Without reluctance he has drank Senna tea, which I got*
> *to stew with prunes . . . & Dr. M. desiring his Ears to*
> *be bathed with Sea water, he took a cup of it whenever I*
> *bad him, only saying it was* not good. *He also got a dose*
> *of Epsom Salts & the Doctor wishing much he shd. get*
> *a Calomile Pill, or rather a* powder'd grain, *he took it*
> *last night & this day Salts, neither have sickened him &*
> *just now have the desired effect. One from the Calomile*
> *I hope will be against worms, of which he has some of*
> *the symptoms. I have no doubt but he will shortly be*
> *clear & better than ever. . . . A spot is also on his head,*
> *but dry & I hope will not now increase, if it shd. it must*
> *be promoted not restrained. . . . A change of air with*
> *plenty of fresh buttermilk, I have not a doubt, will soon*
> *recover his beauty, for he has lost little else, tho' on*
> *coming here* [Cabin Hill] *on Monday, they all exclaimed*
> *Belfast wd. kill Tom & glad they were to get him back.*[26]

It is not surprising that in reply to all this Dr. Drennan
should send some advice.

> *I think Thomas will get the better of this complaint, but*
> *I would have you pursue with him a* regular plan *for*
> *some time. Once a week I would give him at bed-time a*

*grain of calomil mixed with some powdered sugar, or a
little currant jelly. The next morning he ought to take
some physic, such as a breakfast cup full of Salt water,
adding a little common water, or a little cream of tartar
makes it more palatable. Or a dessert spoonful of Epsom
Salts dissolved in broth. We are accustomed here to have
salts, such as the Rochelle, saturated with the aerated
water, which renders them very palatable, and it is sold
in half-pint or pint bottles. In the intermediate days of
the week, I would wish him to take, every morning, a
cup of Salt Water diluted with some common water, not
so much as to operate as a physic, or if so very gently,
for I think much physicking bad, and tho' some may be
necessary at present, it would be better when the inflammation abated, that his skin should be soft and perspir-
able, which purging prevents, but which would prevent
a return of such eruptions more than any other means.
With respect to external applications, I think the fewer
the better. The wax-kernels are little glandular swellings
proceeding from the parts broken out, and will disappear
when they are healed—but with respect to the spot on
his head, I do think that it shd. be healed, as it is very
apt to be communicated from a small spot all over the
head, and I have seen so often the efficacy of a little Tar
ointment in such cases, that I think you might try it,
either getting a small box of it prepared by the apothecary or making a little yourself with some lard, or honey,
and rubbing it well on the place, after cutting the hair
off . . . I don't apprehend worms in this case.*[27]

One is rather amazed at the confident manner in which this
diagnosis is made in the absence of the patient.

In spite of, or because of, all this doctoring the ears began
to heal:

*Mrs. Blackley call'd for a few minutes yesterday. She will
tell you she saw Tom confined to the House, in a Night*

*Cap, & Wrapper, with a scabbed face, which yet, being a Mother, she kissed; & his Ears begin to itch very much, I hope they are mending, but he scratches them in his sleep & adds to his bad appearance . . . By the bye, when you say you do not like much physic yet order Salts once a week & sea water every Day, I think you are not very sparing, he takes all willingly but says he likes his Papa's best, meaning the Imperial of which he is very fond. I wish him well for his mind's sake as well as his body, for if he does not get rambling once more both will grow soft & effeminate.*[28]

At any rate Tom was well enough to be critical about his tea! 'This morning he told me he did not like Ramsay's tea —he wished I wd. get Kennedy's. Upon repeating this I tasted the tea & found I had forgot the sugar, telling him that was the fault. "Well then," said he, "you should speak to me the same way you do to Cousin." "How is that?" "You ask *her* if her tea is right".'[28]

Dr. Drennan continued to prescribe, and instructions arrived about single grains of James' Powder, ten or twelve drops of antimonial wine taken in a little whey, a Burgundy pitch plaster, and a little sulphur and treacle mixed.[29] Mrs. M'Tier wrote reassuringly to Sarah:

*Your Boy is perfectly well . . . Calves feet jelly is now preparing for his one oClock dinner, his breakfast was warm milk, just from the cow, on bread. His dinner now a little flesh, a little Wine; at seven bread & butter & a cup of something like tea, & to all this he frequently chuses supper of barley & good milk, so that I think the White Rose will soon be again a red one—an appellation Tom is very fond of but which wd. not be just at present. I believe* [she added] *it was the worms that dimmed him.*[30]

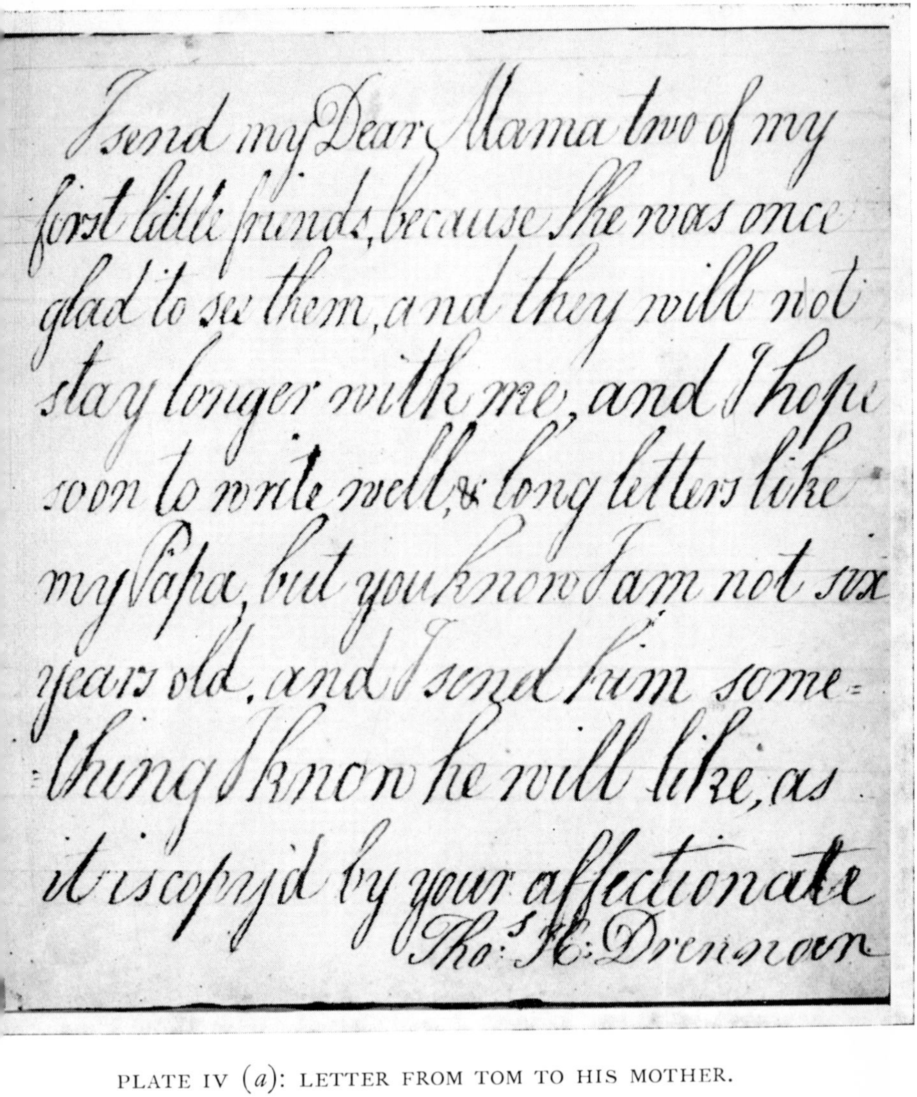

I send my Dear Mama two of my first little friends, because She was once glad to see them, and they will not stay longer with me, and I hope soon to write well, & long letters like my Papa, but you know I am not six years old, and I send him something I know he will like, as it is copyd by your affectionate
Tho:<sup>s</sup> H. Drennan

PLATE IV (*a*): LETTER FROM TOM TO HIS MOTHER.

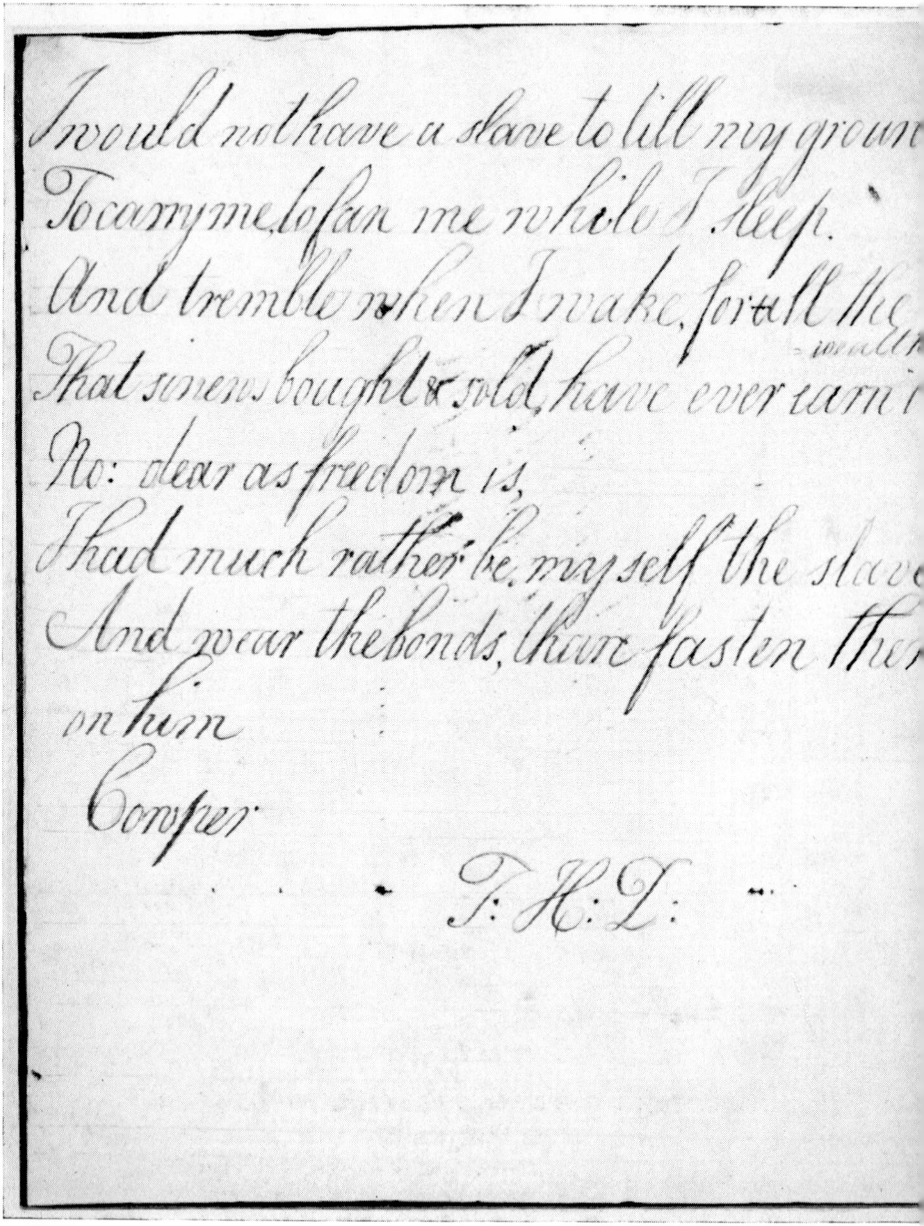

I would not have a slave to till my ground
To carry me, to fan me while I sleep.
And tremble when I wake, for all the
That sinews bought & sold, have ever earn'd
No: dear as freedom is,
I had much rather be, myself the slave
And wear the bonds, thaire fasten them
on him
Cowper

T. H. L.

PLATE IV (b).

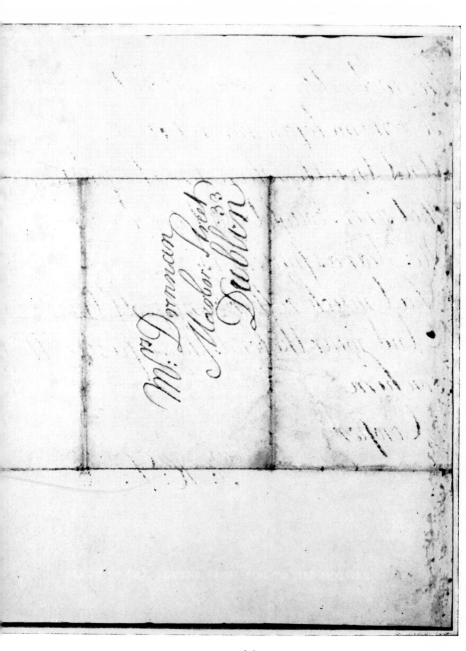

PLATE IV $(c)$.

Tom's convalescence was slow and the strain of nursing had had an unusual effect on Matty, in writing to her Dr. Drennan alludes to signs of worry; the letter is worth quoting at length because of the medical details it contains.

*My Dear Sister,*
*. . . You are paying a heavy Tax for the pleasure Thomas has afforded you, but your writing in low spirits about him has had the effect of keeping ours up, and we both attribute your alarm, in part, to your maternal anxiety about him. . . I am not sure that you are not too anxious about opening medicine which generally, after their effect, add to the restrained state, and make a recurrence to them appear necessary. When the children had this tendency I found it much better to use* clysters *occasionally, which I always gave myself, for it is an excellent way of opening the bowels, but generally fails by being not administered properly. A trial of these ought, I think, to be made, and I would confide more to an apothecary, or even his apprentice, than to even an experienced old woman to give it properly. A cup-full of mutton-broth with a dessert spoonfull of common salt in it, or of epsom salt in powder, thrown up gently so as to be retained for a quarter of an hour, would probably produce a laxative motion, and this should be increased in the* quantity *or made stronger of the salt as found necessary, and I should not be satisf'd at it failing the first time, which it generally does by mismanagement, but have it try'd again and again, till the operation & and patient become better used to it. I generally used a pewter Syringe to the infant, but this probably would not hold enough of the liquid to affect the bowels. We have bottles made of elastic gum with a pipe fitted in them for the purpose—Mrs. Bruce has one of this kind which she got in Dublin for injecting into Sam's ears; which however he probably took to Scot-*

*land with him. Perhaps by enjuiry from the Apothecary you could get such, and at any rate I wish you to get your Apothecary to administer a proper injection every second or third day. Purging medicines, and particularly calomel, will affect the countenance & in sleep the features will look worse. . . . With respect to Worm cakes, you may depend on it, that calomel is the principal ingredient, and generally combined with jalap. I can therefore, have no objection, with Dr. Mateer's sanction to his trying any of these medicines in moderate quantity. . . . You do not speak of any general, or local swelling or hardness in his belly, or any pain upon pressure, particularly on the right side, & I therefore conclude he is without such symptoms. On considering the matter as well as I can, both as Father and Physician, I am inclined, through you, to ask our good Friend Dr. Mateer, whether any* invigorating, strengthening *course of medicines might not contribute to increase the tone of the alimentary canal, which perhaps requires such medicines, and by bracing the whole frame, might lessen the irritability, humble the feverishness and perhaps give the system power to throw out on the surface any peccant humour that may now disorder some of the internal organs. Might not a wine glass full of infusion of the Bark rendered palatable with syrup of orange peel or violet, taken twice a day be of service. Do you give him any Wine? Might not a glass or two in the Day be worthy of trial. . . . Have you ever got him to take a Dessert spoonfull of Castor oil which I think he could easily be made to swallow on a little broth. But, on the whole, considering he has for a considerable time been using laxative medicines, I should be inclined to try the effect of* clysters *given by the apothecary, and some bracing medicine, such as decoction or infusion of bark, with as much Wine, or Wine and Water, in the day as you think he can safely bear, and two or three sweet*

*oranges if they are to be had, or some tamarinds if he*
*likes them. . . . You may read what I have said to Dr. M.*
*who will receive my sentiments with the candour to which*
*they are entitled, and will judge to what extent anything*
*I say, in my present perturbation of mind, may be use-*
*ful. . . . My fear chiefly at present is that he may be*
*weakened too much, and that a bracing, restorative, in-*
*vigorating course is become proper, not by loading his*
*stomach with jellies, etc. but by bracing medicines taken*
*regularly for some time. Dear Matty, we no doubt will*
*hear from you. Nancy, I am sure is much alarmed. But*
*we hope the best, and if the worst should happen, I hope,*
*we shall be resigned to the will of God. Grant him, O*
*God, to recover his health & make us happy.*
*Yrs. ever —*
*W.D.*[31]

Mercifully, the child recovered, and Mrs. M'Tier,
resuming her habitual confidence, wrote that 'he has finished
a 2d. paper of powders—is now getting bark &, prepared in
flannel waistcoats, I mean to recall his roses at C.H. in a day
or two'.[32] When they were settled at Cabin Hill she reported
that Tom continued to improve. The weather being 'remarkably cold & damp' he had not so far been out of doors,

*yet his spirits never flags among his old women who he*
*terms boys. . . . He has so many things to take I do not*
*know when to get them all in. In the mornings he gets*
*bread with hot milk from the cow to make him fat. At*
*noon he gets bark to make him strong, after some fadge,*
*or barley bread, with honey spread on it to keep him open*
*—at dinner beef, & wine & water to make him robust—*
*malt squeezed in when I can & as he does not now sleep*
*in the Day his tea is his supper, & he is asleep at 9 o'clock*
*. . . In short I hope he will never alarm me again!*[33]

These weeks of nursing strengthened, if that were possible, the bond between Thomas and his Aunt. It would seem that he still slept in her bed, for Mrs. M'Tier relates how 'the other morning in bed (a time we have a good deal of conversation)' she mentioned that in time she would grow old and deaf like his Grandmother. 'His heart fill'd, he made the long lip & said, "O no Aunt Ateer, don't grow old, don't". "But I must grow old or die young" [she replied]. "Do die young then, do die young & I will die with you, young too." '[33] This interlude of sadness soon ended, and in the next letter we read that Tom had assured her that 'God sent his Angels to take care of him when he slept & that he wd. meet me in Heaven, but (with this hope I suppose) he wanted much to know if a Soul had a *face*'.[34] On another occasion, after declaring that he would meet his Aunt in Heaven, he wondered where they would sleep; Mrs. M'Tier's suggestion of a cloud was unsatisfactory, for, says Tom, 'if it rains we will drop down'.[35] As with every child of his age these profundities presented a lively, if transient, interest.

There is little direct evidence of the kind of early religious teaching that Thomas received. Dr. Drennan was, I imagine, a more conventionally religious person than his sister: he once described himself to Matty as being 'sincerely religious, tho' I cannot say I go much farther than what the belief of one God—the Maker and *Preserver* of all things—must suggest to every attentive mind'.[36] Their father had been a dissenting minister and there is every indication that his memory and ideals were venerated in every respect by his son. We know that Dr. Drennan conducted family prayers with his household[37] and we have seen the hymn which he composed and expected Thomas to learn by heart.

Mrs. M'Tier's approach was less conventional, but with both of them religious belief found expression in a strongly marked independence of thought, and a passion for liberty, encouraged by the rational philosophy that had reached the North of Ireland from the universities of Edinburgh and Glasgow, and also directly from France. For example, the Scottish philosopher Dugald Stewart, who at that very time was educating the young Harry Temple — later Lord Palmerston, Foreign Secretary, Prime Minister—in his home in Edinburgh, had been known to Dr. Drennan since the days when they were both students at the university. But, with all this intellectualism there was a very human approach to religion, and Tom, like every fortunate child, learnt about the fatherhead of God through his own happy family relationships. Very likely too, Matty read to him such sentences as these from Mrs. Barbauld's *Hymns in Prose*:

There is little need that I should tell you of
God, for everything speaks of Him.
Every field is like an open book; every painted
flower has a lesson written on its leaves.
Every murmuring brook hath a tongue: a voice is
in every whispering wind.[38]

There is one charming story which illustrates how naturally Tom viewed religious subjects. On being asked by a chance inquirer what he intended to call a little pet dog, he had replied 'J: Ct.'—to use Mrs. M'Tier's respectfully abbreviated form. The story had been repeated to her, and anxious to hear it herself she 'had thrown baits for Tom not to *fear* repeating it, but he never dropt a word like it. He has a Hymn of Watts where "the sweet (& as he terms it the Darling) child" is mentioned, but from this I do not think it could arise'.[39]

Meanwhile, in spite of months of illness, Dr. Drennan continued to press the importance of education. 'I hope,' he wrote, 'Tom learnt his Lessons during his illness. I think under so good a mistress he will be able to read English at four years old.'[40] And again: 'Does he yet discover any turn, or bent of Mind, any hobby horse of this sort? Which

of his senses, next to that of taste, is the one he would seem
to cultivate most? William, from his fondness of pins and
buttons, will, we fear, be a Taylor'.[41] To this more or less
serious query Mrs. M'Tier replied, in a letter to Sarah, that
Tom's 'particular taste is not only for *eating* but making hot
baps, to which chew'd bread, wet paper, clay, etc. is so constantly converted that I have no doubt he ought to be made
a *baker*, & as Wm promises well for a taylor the *Doctor* may
be very happy in the prospect of such useful occupations
in a Land where such only secures from starvation'.[42] This
delight in modelling and in the use of dough for the purpose
is another interesting eighteenth century commentary on
so-called modern educational theories.

On one cold December afternoon when Mrs. M'Tier was
cosily enjoying what she termed 'Cabin Hill indulgence—
an afternoon nap' she was rudely awakened by a voice 'more
loud than usual' calling ' "Aunt Ateer, Aunt, a letter for
Tommy & something else," which something else [a book]
being most relished, the letter was little attended to for some
time'.[42] The letter has not been preserved, and it is probable
that the book accompanying it was a New Year gift to
Tom from his father, for in all staunchly presbyterian
families it was the New Year, and not Christmas, that was
celebrated with festivities. At this particular New Year Miss
Young had decided to give a Bible to John Anderson, the
gardener at Cabin Hill. The book, which cost her one guinea,
lay on her table, and 'by way of tryal', she asked Tom 'to
read what was in the first Leaf. "Holy Bible," says Tom.
"That's my good Boy, I wonder who printed it, can you see
who it is printed for?" "Printed — printed for Chas. Fox,"
was the reply. "For Fox," repeated she, "what more?" "At
commands of Miss Young for John Anderson," read Tom.
"You little rascal, how dare you tell such fibs," scolded the
old lady, but Tom, looking up at her with the sweetest
smile, reassuringly declared, " 'twas only make believe,

Cousin".[43] Astonishingly clever 'make believe' for a child not yet four years old. In the same letter Mrs. M'Tier writes:

> *I am just come in from playing shinny on a clear, cold day, which evidently agrees so well with him that I acknowledge I encounter its dangers, and trust his flannel waistcoat more than the fireside. I shall not be rash, but I cannot give up my system of cold bracing preventing colds, & every morning I splash his face & ears well in water . . . his color glows—in the severest weather he hates the fire, not the least cough, nor cold in his head which, while he was confined he never wanted. His [grows] apace & you need not suspect either his memory, judgement or ability to read in a natural time. He puzzled me this morning by desiring me to tell him all the bad beasts & serpents Downpatrick had, & insisted I once told him Downpatrick took them all from Ireland.*[43]

This is, of course, a reference to the legend that St. Patrick banished all reptiles from Ireland and, though Tom had confused Downpatrick (a town in Co. Down) with the Saint's name, the anecdote illustrates what a receptive mind he had, and the far from childish information that he stored in it. An Aunt who could so acceptably, and at the age of sixty-plus, combine shinny and St. Patrick must indeed have been, as Dr. Drennan remarked, 'a good mistress'.

Tom's health had quite recovered, but scarlet fever, chincough and measles were prevalent, and Matty was anxious to protect him from infection. Dr. Drennan writes of a new method of treating scarlet fever used successfully by Dr. Gregory of Edinburgh, which entailed 'throwing cold water on the patients when in a dry, burning heat'.[44] An outbreak of croup caused great alarm, and, as a precaution, tobacco was burned in chafing dishes in the shrubberies at Cabin Hill.[45]

In the house in Dublin illness had come with fatal results: John, the year-old brother whom Tom had never seen, died in the spring. Tom's oft discussed return to his parents was now hastily fixed, Matty being asked to accompany him so that she could keep house for her brother while Sarah, in order to revive her saddened spirits, went on a visit to her parents in Shropshire. Writing to her sister-in-law on the day she heard of little John's death, Matty quoted old Dr. Mateer as saying of Tom, with deep affection, 'there are few like him' and she continues:

*Few indeed—perfect in temper, happy in spirits— pleasing & pleased by natural untaught obedience flow- ing from love and never exacted — in form, face & manner a Nature's gentleman. Any defficiencys must be laid to my charge—& I begin to regret I did not give him more instructions, as they wd. not have been thrown away, but his natural charms were so attractive, not only to me but very other person who knew him, of every station, that I did not desire to give them any tinseled forms. You will I fear find him deficient in several forms, which I pass'd over at home, from a dislike of formality, but by doing so you cannot expect them abroad.*[46]

She goes on to explain that 'his soft, silver tones are quite changed to harsh Northern ones & even an affectation of speaking broad, from which he was pretty well preserved till lately. In reading, to prevent the *extreme* we are here apt to go into by sounding the "a" broad, I have made him sound it "e"—yet this had not preserved him from contagion, tho' I think it will help you to reform it. Indeed I am sure he will very soon cease from anything ungenteel, he has a variety of well adapted words & never misapplys one, tho' on the *first* using—he can read tolerably all Mrs. B[arbauld]'s little books sent by his Father'.

The old ladies were desolate at the thought of losing the dear child. 'Miss B. is very poorly indeed & her nerves so disordered that Tom's going away was never hinted at that it did not raise such a volcano of wind we have lived in an internal storm... Miss Young confined to her room & my poor Mother grumbling at my going so far. But I tell them all had I not taken such a step two years ago they wd. have lost all that pleasure they have since had with Tom.'[47]

There is little mention of Mrs. M'Tier's own feelings. After all, it was she who would take Tom to Dublin, and while, no doubt, she secretly hoped they would return together, the uncertainty of the future may have been temporarily blurred by the pleasure of the present, for she could look forward with legitimate pride to restoring him to his parents with all the evidence of her loving care. 'Whatever You & my Brother think most for your *pleasure*,' she writes to Sarah, 'I am willing to do. I cd. set off with Tom tomorrow if I knew of a partner in a Chaise.' As it was, they set off by the Mail Coach on an April morning three weeks later, Tom spending one of his last evenings at the circus with the Sinclaire family. Good Cousin Young 'gave us 10 guineas to bear our expenses & a charge to return to her— but this [adds Matty courageously] as seemth best for *him* not M.M.[47]

Tom was just four years and one month old; two years exactly had elapsed since the memorable journey when she had brought him to Belfast. During that time his father had seen him once; we can judge of the ardent anticipation with which his mother awaited the arrival of her darling first-born son.

# Chapter IV: Four years old

**T**HERE is no description at all of the journey nor of the great arrival in Dublin; of Matty's triumphant presentation of her charge, and of the loving welcome from his parents that awaited Tom; and there is very little about two excited little fellows—scampering in and out of rooms, and up and down the stairs of the tall house in Marlborough Street. In a brief and hasty note to his sister Nancy, written a few hours after the arrival of the travellers, Dr. Drennan has only time to state that they reached Dublin safely, and that Tom has as yet 'scarcely got acquaintance with his Father and Mother, but with Wm. he is prefectly at home and they have been riding the hobby-horse ever since Thomas came'. As for Mrs. M'Tier she 'looks as well as I have seen her, and all the difference I could perceive is a deficiency in the Teeth.'[1]

After enjoying her Thomas for barely one month, Sarah set off on the visit to her parents. The crossing to Holyhead was bad and on receiving news of her safe landing Dr. Drennan wrote to her that 'I have employed myself this morning going round our Friends [and he names the various streets] to announce to them that you had passed through Purgatory, and were probably now in Abram's bosom, that is in your good Father's arms'. Mrs. M'Tier took up the reins of office. She followed Sarah's practice of going to the market for provisions, and within a week Dr. Drennan was telling his wife that James [another manservant] was engaged in colouring the walls of the staircase, hall and drawing-room 'under her direction'. 'James,' he adds, 'is more at home in the new administration than Kitty, who does not like the marketing, and a mistake of two old Bantam hens for large chickens has led to comparisons of the present with the late Mistress.'[2] Evidently Matty had not yet got the measure of Dublin 'chicken-women'! However, on the whole everything ran very smoothly, and Dr. Drennan's letters to Sarah are full of affection, of items of gossipy news about patients, and of descriptions of entertainments given by relatives and friends for the grass-widower and his sister. At one party the 'cold ham was so so nicely sliced, & spread on the plates so evenly, that it appeared like painting' and, though Dr. Drennan was not himself so rude as to count the slices, his lady companion discovered surreptitiously that there were twelve on each plate! At another party their hostess 'was rather discom-posed at dinner by a very fine salmon being sent up but half boiled. It was ordered again to the kitchen and came up again at the close of the meal'. Apparently the courses were conveniently interchangeable.

More important, however, are reassuring remarks about the children's welfare, though even at this stage 'Tom at times looks poorly, but is now taking camomile Tea at my sister's direction', and again—'Tom is very thin'. Neverthe-less, his spirits were gay as ever: he is reported as being 'an exceeding great favorite of the Fair. He is at present in high spirits, marching with little Thomas Touche while William is the drummer. He likes to walk out with me, as well as I do to take him [admits the proud father], and he has got an acquaintance at several houses already. Old Mrs. Ford is anxious to see him from the account she has heard of his conversation with the Men in the garden'. Another lady, finding Mrs. M'Tier from home when she drew up at the house to pay her call, 'took Thomas into the carriage and chatted with them'. And there is this lovely picture of Dr. Drennan returning on foot from visiting a patient some distance away, 'bearing our son and heir upon my back, the only condition I could assent to becoming a beast of burden. The weather is so warm now [June] I was unwilling to let him walk back'.[2] But there are no emotional outbursts as on p. 23, and none of the 'Tommy anecdotes' that filled Mrs. M'Tier's letters from Belfast. In one of the last latters to Sarah this ominous sentence occurs: 'Nothing is fixed respecting Tom's return [to Belfast], on the whole, with your concurrance I would wish him to have the benefit of the country as much as possible.'[2] To which Sarah replied: 'A letter from you to-day and another from my sister this morning have made me most happy. All well and doing well in that beloved home which I long to see again. Dear Tom, you both tell me, is very thin; whatever will promote his health I shall cheerfully accede to, though I cannot help sighing at the thought that I know and can see so little of my child'.[2]

Sarah arrived home sometime in June and there followed days of family festivities to celebrate the re-union: a large party of friends and relations went to see *The Merry Wives of Windsor*—we are not told that Tom was taken—and at an evening party given by Mrs. Godley—the lady who had called Tom into her carriage—Matty, according her her brother, 'looked as well, and was as well dressed, as I *ever* remember to have seen her, which at her time of life is no mean compliment'.

But eventually the fateful question had to be faced. Bearing mind Dr. Drennan's remark about 'the benefit of the country' and Sarah's reply, it would seem that it was she particularly, who could not bear to face another period of separation, so in due course the following letter was despatched to Nancy Drennan in Belfast:

*After two or three Cabinet Conferences it is now finally determined that Tom is for some time to remain behind, and that William may possibly ask for a month or two the protection of your roof. The chief reason that influenced us in this was his Mother's wish not to estrange Tom's* *too great a length of time from his parents* [sic]. *We do not think that the Country will agree with him better than the warmth of the City in Winter, and during the remainder of the Summer we think that his body & mind may be as usefully exercised in Dublin, that he will not want fruit if necessary, and that Sea-bathing is more conveniently to be had by his Aunt's* jaunting Car, if it be found, on trial, to agree with him, which it will take some time to know. He is at present thin, but I think not thinner than when he came up, and has good appetite, excellent spirits & great activity. My Sister will feel the separation very sensibly and much longer than he will do, who finds amusement from every new object, but she seems satisfy'd in the propriety of our resolution & to accede to it as the best, knowing that a child certainly of delicate constitution is perhaps better under the same roof of his Father and Physician . . . The truth is, neither of us liked the idea of my Sister returning without either one or other of the children, and she, I believe of herself, proposed to take William on a visit to his Friends. They are at present busy by my side, at a bowl of gooseberries & milk—in great glee & enjoyment.*[3]

Poor Matty! All her courage and affection were mobilised to meet this bitter disappointment. Perhaps it was only at that moment of decision that she realised how tenderly she loved Tom, and how necessary he had become to her happiness. But—'she is satisfied in the propriety of our resolution, and accedes to it'. One wonders if the next remark about the advisability of the delicate child being under the same roof as 'his Father and Physician' was not more in keeping with Dr. Drennan's sentiments than his sister's'.

---

* A sister of Sarah's who lived in Dublin.

So, on a warm July morning, Mrs. M'Tier set off for
home with William, now 3 years old. It was a two-day
journey—'owing to a delay at Hillsborough for want of
horses and when we got them the unfortunate brutes had
been in Belfast that day before', so they did not reach their
destination till 10 p.m. The child, though 'just awake out of
a sound sleep' was immediately presented to his waiting
Aunt Ann [Nancy], she who was to be his 'adopted Mother'
for the next few weeks. 'He behaved well & from the day he
left you to this night, has never cried, nor appeared dis-
satisfied. My Mother and everyone in the house appears
greatly pleased, *tho*' they do not think him *like* Tom . . . He
never disturbed me thro' the night & at 9 oClock I heard
him repeat the word Belfast a dozen times . . . In short no
child could have behaved better, not one in a thousand so
well.'[4] So wrote Mrs. M'Tier of the journey. Certainly Dr.
Drennan had two very adaptable little boys.

Poor William—we can only hope that he was unaware of
the heavy handicap with which, as a substitute for Tom, he
encountered his northern relations. Actually, he was quite
different from Tom—a sturdy, hot-tempered little fellow,
with a great charm of his own, which, however, did not
include Tom's acute sensitivity for the feelings of other
people. At Cabin Hill Miss Biggar had been counting the
weeks during Matty's absence and 'dreaming repeatedly of
Tom', and when Nancy informed her of William's proposed
visit 'she made no objection, but desired her to let Mrs.
Drennan know she was very sorry *indeed* at the new
arrangem't', which observation Matty could not refrain from
passing on to Dublin. When William was taken to pay his
respects to the two ladies Mrs. M'Tier wrote that 'Miss Y.
received us well, and the child *most kindly*; Miss B. as well
as she cou'd, but she had to leave the room twice, and were
I to describe her feelings *you* wou'd say, as you did of Tom's
sympathetic tears, they were *affectation*, just as much so in
one case as the other'.[5]

Try as she would to demonstrate her impartiality by much
kindness to William, Mrs. M'Tier's thoughts were constantly in Dublin with the absent child. This is the first little
note she wrote to Tom after her return to Belfast:

> *My dear Tom*
>     *William is grown quite good as I hope you will
> continue to be, & do everything your Papa & Mama bid
> you, for you know I always told you to love them better
> than any other person, & particularly your* Mama—*and
> I know you will. She will be so good to you, & remember
> never to tell a lie, I shall love you all my life & often
> send you letters and good things. We got Strawberries
> from C: Hill today & Wm longs to go there, with yr.
> affect'.*
>
>                                   *Aunt.*[6]

One can read a good deal between those lines.

A week later she wrote to her brother that William 'continues as good as possible & highly delighted with everything, tho' from the bad weather and the broken up state of
the ground before my Mo'rs. door, he has got little out'.
In a day or two she hopes to have him at Cabin Hill, but
everything there reminds her so forcibly of Tom: 'I have
been so long used,' she continues, 'to see something pretty
near me, particularly when I lie down & awake, that I miss
my *dearest* Boy very sadly since I came out; every spot
reminds me of him & the little interesting prattle we had in
them—particularly from 9 till 10 at night, when we both
relished a blazing ingle & each other, and *this* it was which
made him not relish a lonely room. [Dr. Drennan had
strongly disapproved of this stimulated sentimentality.] I
wrote to him last week but will now add to this letter &
direct it to *himself*, conveying his first seal-breaking pleasure.
I hope *you* won't do it for him. Heaven bless my little
angel'.[7]

As for Thomas, in spite of the assurances that he found 'amusement from every new object' he made little secret of his longings for Aunt M'Tier. Dr. Drennan gives this charming description of the receipt of one of her letters:

*We received your Dundalk Epistle* [written during the journey to Belfast], *or rather more truly Tom received it as he hurry'd down on the wings of love to the hall-door, shouting—a Letter from Aunt M'Tier—and when it was read to him he seemed pleased, but not satisfy'd, as all lovers are on receiving letters from their mistresses, but what little you did say seemed to make a favourable impression, and the truth is, he has felt very* uncomfortable *since you left us, nor has he had insincerity enough to disguise it, even in the presence of Father and Mother. He has very frequently, after a hearty yawn at the company present, burst suddenly into an exclamation, 'I shd.* like *to be at Cabin Hill'* (and his like *may be well interpreted* love). *Particularly about bed-time he says longingly, 'I wish my Aunt was here,' but still he resigns himself complacently to the necessity of the case ... Indeed you may conceive to what an extent his affection reaches in every thing relating to you when this morning he said he did not like the Utensil below the bed, and requested his mother to get him in future (saving your favour) his Aunt's pot de chambre, for he would make use of no other ... The period of* lasting *mental pain is not felt by children* [how little did he understand], *tho' they are very early susceptible of pleasures of the heart & affections; and the chief blessing of life, the pleasure of Hope, he at present feels very sensibly, as he often repeats' 'how many days, Papa, till we go in a* gig *to Belfast, when we shall drive time about'. This gig and this journey is the early blossom of his imagination, and gives him already a foretaste of the future. William is a boy more of*

PLATE V: THE LINEN HALL, BELFAST.

*the* senses, *than the* sensibilities, *and will enjoy the present without incorporating with it either the past or future.*[8]

When the letter, specially addressed to Tom, arrived it made, according to Dr. Drennan,

*the impression you wished. He looked very grave, and then smiled, and then laughed as if his vanity were tickled, and I think his ambition to read and write will be more and more excited. He is in good health and sleeps on the whole, I believe, better than in the same bed wtih anyone. He is a great dreamer, at least whenever he wakens it is to tell us his dream of the night which generally hovers over Cabin Hill. Kitty the nurse-maid has left us, and his Mother undresses, and dresses him, hears his night & morning prayer, and kisses him when finished . . . He can build the Country-Inn you bought him without any assistance and works in the garden as much as the weather will allow.*[9]

Such were Sarah's efforts to win the affection of her little son.

From what we can gather from these letters it would seem that Sarah was blessed with a placid nature and considerable practical and intellectual ability. She was an excellent wife to her introspective, over-sensitive husband, and she loved both him and their children dearly. One wonders, though, if she had that quality of spontaneous, glowing affection that Tom's warm little heart demanded. The well-deserved 'whippings' administered by Aunt M'Tier aroused not the slightest hint of resentment because of her overflowing love on which he knew he could always depend, and for which, in those years, he yearned.

Meanwhile, writing of William to her sister-in-law, Matty illustrates very clearly the differences between the two children and her reactions to them:

*Wm. is an extreme fine Boy, & every one thinks so, for both yours have the peculiar good breeding of a frank, good reception at first. Nancy maintains he is a smarter Boy than Tom, and is not only fond of him but admires him much, & ... you cou'd not believe how much strangers and the praise of his Brother has improved him. He is in excellent spirits & never-ceasing talk, yet his former Spirit* [temper] *not yet quite subdued. He has been in a passion of tears twice for no cause & both times whipt into immediate propriety, and this morning narrowly escaped it for flinging away his bread in disdain of its not being Bap. I often think with concern the little care that was taken to correct my temper, or rather how its faults were cherished by the passion of my Mother & the atoning fondness of my Father. Certainly the present times are much more favorable to education even on important matters, & command of temper may be the very best foundation for true politeness & the graces. But, Sarah, to return to your pet. On a wet day he took his seat where Tom did, on Miss Young's bed & near her basket. She told him she was a poor lame woman & that Tom always helped her to walk, & several hours after he really, of himself, went to her with his arm to help her to the drawing room, so she thinks yr. children wonders. Tom, however, she dwells on day & night, for her dreams of him are frequent & most particularly related.*[10]

And again to her brother:

*Wm. is a fine Boy, I have him now here* [at Cabin Hill] *with me, and see the necessity of a strict watch over his temper, which is passionate & then imperious to a high degree. I am the only one here he stands in awe of, and I must retain this. I think if he is ever put to school, he will run off, or from an apprenticeship.* [On returning one day from the garden] *he insisted the Door shd. not*

*be locked, he placed himself in the breach, wd. neither go
in nor out, but roared so loud I heard him on the road &,
hurrying up, found him raging in the Hall, & striking
each side of it with a Whip, so that no one cd. go near
him. On hearing I was coming he try'd to cool, but cd.
not get it effected in time to save a whipping & afterwards being put up in his room. On promise of amend-
ment he got out, when he instantly took to his heels down
to the gardener's, nor wd. return 'till it was dark.' I
merely tell you this to show I am not partial.*[11]

In Dublin Tom's health continued to cause anxiety. 'He
has been affected,' writes his Father, 'with feverishness and
for a time want of appetite . . . He requires means to keep his
spirits afloat & I think grows languid and indolent without
some constant entertainment, which I dont think he finds so
much of and in himself as William. [There had been no
difficulty about keeping spirits 'afloat' at Cabin Hill.] At
present he is very wan in his complexion and thin. He looks
out for your presents with ardour, and still runs to the door
for your letters.'[12] To which Matty replied that she 'well
knew Tom's spirits would fail him in Dublin for . . . considering the free range he had here, both for mind and body,
the variety of people & situation with their desire to please
him, it cannot be wondered that he wd. sink for a little in
Marlborough St. without even a story-telling servant, nor
yet able to read for himself, & were it not for the *needless*
expense I often wished he was to go to school, even in the
Winter's Day, as a bracer to both body & mind.'[13] Was there
anyone, Matty may have wondered, in that great tall house,
who would take the child on her knee or sit by him at the
fire, whiling away a long afternoon with an exciting tale of
some strange happening, or a hastily concocted, but no less
enchanting, story about an ordinary little boy? As for a game
of shinney, had anyone in Marlborough Street even heard
of such a thing?

In spite of that strong hint, his parents, desperately anxious to keep Tom with them, decided on sending him for a short visit to some friends who lived not far from Dublin; it was even suggested that William should be brought from Belfast to provide companionship for Tom. Mrs. M'Tier persisted, urging significantly, but without any trace of rancour, that as 'Sarah is now *certain* she can procure *love* when she pleases', Tom should be sent back to her, 'tho',' she adds, 'the *responsibility* is too great for any one but yr. fearless sister ... nor for one moment take expense into consideration—trash in comparison to a smile of my Darlings —that captivating grace hovers particularly over yr. *Boys*.'[14] Obviously she was willing to have both nephews. Presumably this 'expense' relates to outlay on the children's keep in Belfast: I have not discovered any arrangement whereby Dr. Drennan met these costs. Sarah was now pregnant for the fifth time.

At length Matty prevailed, and, overjoyed at the news that Tom was to return to her, she sent him this letter:

*My Dr. Tom,*
      *We are all happy to find yr. Papa & Mama are so good as to let you come so soon again to C: Hill. I am sure you will never forget them again, & how they love you—and we will all be so happy here, and only sorry that your Dear Mama is not with us. And Willy is very fond of C: H: as you are, & everybody loves him for he never cries. And the Robins begin to come to him for I believe they think it is you. I wou'd have sent you money for your own use on the road—but I kept it all to buy yr. little poney, & yr. saddle, & it shall not be larger than a big Dog, & you shall ride to Greenville, & Mr. Gordon's, & I will walk by yr. side every good Day, down & up the Avenue, but you must ask yr. Cousin to give it meat, and you & I will run about the fields, &*

*be very good & very happy, but you are now so big I must get you a Bed for y'rself.*[15]

In September, 1805, Dr. Drennan took Thomas to Belfast. He stayed for a few days and this letter to Sarah reveals his anxiety for the child's health:

*Our children are both happy & enjoying each others company. I trust that Tom will soon get better, tho' my sister M'Tier seemed last night rather flat about him. Ah, dear Sarah we both owe more to that sister's unceasing desires, and endeavours to serve us, more than we shall ever be able to pay.*[16]

Tom quickly began to pick up. When his father returned to Dublin he took William with him, to the great regret of the child and his Aunt Ann. Perhaps it was just as well that the brothers were not required, at that early age, to adjust themselves to sharing the joys of Cabin Hill. William, according to his Aunt M'Tier, did not want to leave

*and therefore, did not like to see Tom, tho' really fond of him, and the Day he arrived, whenever he got an opportunity, gave him a smart stroke on the eye. The men who saw him reproving him, tho' I daresay in a laughing way, he told them he wd. beat him as well as ever he could. Tom slunk off & told a woman on the road he wish'd Willy was gone for he had him in a constant sweat. Though I tell you this to make you laugh mark that Willy is inclined to play the tyrant, & requires that curb which wd. deaden Tom.*[17]

Left to himself Tom revelled in the loving familiarity of everything around him — the house, the old ladies, the servants, the garden and the fields — this was where he felt completely, and happily, at home. Dublin had been new and strange, and after 'Aunt Atier' left, so lonely. And though his sunny and generous nature had sought to 'resign' itself complacently to 'the necessity of the case' there had always been the longing for Cabin Hill. It is said that around four years old a child passes to a new stage of perception and development. Was Tom, during that stay in Dublin, vaguely aware of his Mother's anxiety to win his love, aware perhaps of the smallest—though never expressed—tinge of jealousy towards Aunt M'Tier, aware, in short, of a difficult situation of which he was somehow the centre but which he didn't understand? Was he beginning to sense —again so vaguely—a tension between duty and inclination? He knew that he should love his parents—he who was so acutely sensitive to what other people demanded; during his long absence from them his Aunt had never failed to underline this precept, now her admonitions pursued him in her letters. So he set himself to face 'the necessity of the case', in other words, to try to do what Aunt M'Tier told him. Yet along with this endeavour to love his parents in this strange, lonely Dublin, the alluring picture of getting back to pleasure and happiness shaped itself with growing intensity in his mind. And, in that picture, his father, whom he admired so ardently, would come with him; and they would travel—not by the ordinary coach—but by themselves, in a gig, 'when we shall drive time about'. Truly, 'the pleasure of Hope'—perhaps also the solace of loneliness.

I imagine, but it is only speculation, that the sojourn in Dublin was a period of tension for Thomas, and that only from his Aunt could he derive the sense of security which at that time he needed. Was his declining health due, one wonders, to lack of country air, to some inherent physical weakness, or to this, as yet unresolved, strain? Possibly it was a combination of all three.

Whatever it was, within a fortnight of Dr. Drennan's departure from Cabin Hill, Mrs. M'Tier was able to report that 'no child could have reaped more benefit from charming weather in the Country than Tom has done, his spirits are great, he is *always* cool, out the whole day & his bowels far better than I ever saw them'.[17] Towards the end of that lovely September she took him for a day to Holywood when they spent most of the time 'on the water' and came back to tea by 'moonlight'.

During the next few months there are, happily, only the briefest references to Tom's health, he seems to have completely recovered. He and his Aunt stayed for a few days with Miss Greg where there were other gay and pleasant guests 'all charmed with your Boy, who made himself very agreeable', and after they returned to Cabin Hill there is this long letter ending with the description of a victory bonfire for Trafalgar:

*Tom's health and spirits grow more confirmed every day and his mind more manly. I do not neglect it, tho' he is little, very little, in the house. Never was so delightful an October & November—for here I have never seen once a fog since I left your City, not even now that the mornings are frosty. I breakfast at 9, hear Tom read in the* Testament, *say his prayers & spell, after which he is out till one—comes in then, eats an Egg often, bread & honey or broth, reads* Frank,* *writes & counts. Now is not this fine on* paper *yet I hope all will turn out something before March* [his birthday], *he knows his figures & delights in adding a few together, he knows his letters and can read mine. In the meantime I can trust him to go into any company alone without a fear of the smallest impropriety of behaviour. I sent him to Castle Hill to ask two little Stewarts of his own age here to play with him, he did it at once, but their Mother told him they*

---

* By Maria Edgeworth:

*were not like him for they were shy, and begged he would*
*stay with them. He did so, but told them he wd. not go*
*again unless they came to see him 'till he got his poney*
*& then he wd. ride over and lend it to them. He told me*
*he made all the company laugh four times, but cd. only*
*tell one of the jokes wh. alas! was against himself ...*
*He presided over a Bonfire before the door here the other*
*night in an extacy of enjoyment: Huzzaed, etc. but cd.*
*not be prevailed on to take off his hat, insisting he was*
*the Captain—the Boys received from him pence apiece &*
*the men a glass, for it was so large & well kept up & the*
*news of the 2nd victory not having reached our Neigh-*
*bours, but sent to us by a note from the Chronicle,\* that*
*they sent even from Dundonald to know if C. Hill was*
*on fire & Tom had to answer it was his B.fire for another*
*victory.*[18]

As the dry, sunny autumn turned to winter Matty decided
that she and Tom would go back to Belfast 'that we may both
be the better of some society, & I intend he shall make his
debut at our improved Theatre in the first circle of fashion.
He improves fast in his reading, but I repent having mentioned to you writing & counting, which I have been often
tempted to give up, but knowing how much can be done by
perseverance — & his temper not being soured by it — I yet
go on, believing, contrary to general opinion, that it answers
some good purposes'.[19]

Some days previously Tom had been much interested in
a picture of William Batty, the boy actor better known as
Young Roscius, who was just then, at the age of fifteen,
approaching the height of his phenomenal career. The picture showed the young actor in a highly dramatic posture,
and Matty, anxious to illustrate for Tom some point of

---

* The *Commercial Chronicle*, founded 1805

dramatic art, explained that he was declaiming 'to a distres'd Mother "look how big and strong I am grown, my arm shall support you". His eyes fill'd and when I supposed he might at some time meet his aunt so, he sobbed outright, and when going to bed said, "Aunt I wish to die when you do". "O no, you will live longer." "Then you will always go with me everywhere." "But you will marry and have children, a Wife, and House of yr. own." "Then you will live with me." "No, I wd. be so old yr. wife wd. not be troubled with me." "She shall soon turn out then." '

So much for Matty's efforts to inculcate in Tom an appreciation of dramatic art. We are tempted to think that she was rather tactless in repeating to his parents stories which showed so clearly where the source of his security was to be found, but it was her intense interest in the child which left her, at times, heedless of other people's feelings.

In Belfast anxieties as well as gaiety awaited Mrs. M'Tier. Old Dr. Mateer, who had 'scourged' the top so successfully for Tom's delight, was seriously ill, and her aged mother was becoming increasingly weaker. Another year passed without any specific mention of Christmas, though on December 25th Tom and his Aunt dined at Doctor Mateer's

*with the withered remains of the family party & some odd young ones to help out...It went off well & greatly to Tom's satisfaction, who delights in company, and a set for him to dance with being formed & the Piana [sic] playing, he went through it very tolerably with some grace & an exstacy of pleasure never damped 'till 9 when his heart fill'd & he hid it by a kiss to Mrs. Mateer & left us smiling. What a happiness to himself and others is this angelic temper, contradiction should seldom, very seldom wound it, till it has gained a strength not be injured. I hate thwarting children & they are ill educated that require much of it.*[21]

How wise she was as regards both her discipline and her education! It is well to recall that between us and the expression of these sentiments lies the long Victorian era with its record of supposed repression. Like all true educators Mrs. M'Tier understood the difference between discipline and arbitrary authority: it was not Thomas only, but 'children' that she hated 'thwarting'. She had no qualms about discipline: William she had unhesitatingly 'whipt into immediate propriety' and she wrote again about this second nephew that no one but herself had tried to restrain his temper, yet there was no one he liked better. Tom, too, she disciplined, though in a different manner; even in the very first days in Belfast she would not sit by him till he went to sleep at night, lest he should grow to demand the attention, but she knew well that what was necessary to 'curb' the one child would have 'deadened' the other. 'Seldom, but very seldom'—and then at intolerable cost to herself—was it necessary to wound Tom's 'angelic temper', and we shall see the occasions becoming fewer and fewer.

Family anxiety was not permitted to curtail Tom's share of New Year festivities. His Aunt wrote that he 'is becoming the fashion and much sought for in Donegall Place [the centre of Belfast wealth and gaiety]. Mrs. T. Sinclaire took him to a Puppet show, where he

> greatly amused the company. His delight is a party . . .
> but except to a friendly one at Dr. M's or Mr. Greg's &
> till 9 he does not go. The last day we dined at Greg's,
> with a good many men, Cunningham went up to see his
> wife, & Tom, having placed himself in his chair, was
> told he must give a toast. He inquired 'a Man or a
> Woman', a Lady, said Robt. Davis, the handsomest and
> most agreeable you know. 'Mrs. T. Sinclaire', without the
> slightest hesitation; a general smile, which at length
> became a loud laugh, may be accounted for when you

*know that Davis has long entertain'd a great tho' blame-
less attacht: to this woman. Fortunately Tom was at such
a distance from everyone but* Davis *that no prompting
cd. be suspected. I said I was greatly obliged to the family
& that lately, on being asked for a* friend *he gave Tom
Sinclaire, & said he had carried him home himself one
bad night. He was next desired to give a friend & named
Dr. Mateer, got much credit for his selection. At the shew
he was asked to take out a little girl whose friends wanted
to exhibit her perfect dancing; he immediately complied
and hopped his best ... This sweet compliance in my
Darling gains universal admiration. He is just returned
from Dr. Mateer's, by* himself, *inquiring what sort of a
night he had, for he is very low.*[22]

There must have been a murmur of regret from
Dublin at Tom's continued absence from home and of
caution as to his up-bringing, for in a letter to Sarah there
is this somewhat harsh-sounding assurance:

*I agree with you in what you say of Tom & also that it
may be a loss to him (for a short time) the separation
from his Parents & particularly his Brother. But everything is mixed. Rejoice that he is at present well & happy
—*perfectly *well—& that his mind is of that lovely tex-
ture which will ever be attached to those of similar
dispositions; & when* home *becomes more attractive, by
variety & boyish liberty of which he at present enjoys so
much more than he can do in Dub: , it will have every
charm for him. The attention of strangers & even Servants here affords him much pleasure, with you the latter
were quite deficient in attractions for children, but he will
soon be above these & his Brother will take place of every
companion ... I shall attend to all you say, for there will
be little trouble in keeping the lovely mind of this captivating boy clear of improper impressions at the* age *he*

*will be with me, & I never try'd to inforce one that I
did not succeed. Of the effect of this five year old* [he
was still only four] *let the voice of others (less partial)
judge. They will* not *pronounce him a prodigy — but
everyone announces him the most agreeable child they
ever saw & that is just up to my highest wish now, practical goodness hereafter compleates it.*[23]

Another instance of her wisdom. 'When his home becomes
more attractive', when, in other words, Tom outgrows the
childish joys at that moment so essential to him, then he will
be happy in the more serious, conventional company of his
parents. But for the present he must dance about, he must
play with people—even if they be adults—he must give
rein to his vivid thoughts and enjoy a varied life. How much
more exciting, for example, to this particular child, were
Cunningham Greg's uproarious parties, than the genteel
card-playing evenings so much appreciated by Tom's
parents.

This letter ends with the following significant reference to
old Mrs. Drennan: 'My poor Mother spent a wretched
night, the cough & defluxion allows no sleep, night or day,
nor can she take any nourishment than a raw Egg in her
drink. God relieve her'. The next brief note announced her
death—'This day at 3 o'clock she expired & with so little
struggle that I held her hand to the last. I sent Tom to C.H.
at 2 to-day'.[24] No doubt the joys of the farmyard would
chase away any morbid thoughts. Before Tom returned to
Belfast dear Dr. Mateer had also passed away.

In mourning for his Grandmother Matty considered 'it
better management to die [sic] his brown coat black than
buy a new one of that color. It is done well & he looks well
in it. In the summer he shall have a newer & better, with
long sleeves and suitable Shirts'. There was much business
to transact following the old lady's death, and Tom was
left a good deal to the care and company of other people.

An invitation to go to the theatre with the Gregs was welcomed, for, Mrs. M'Tier wrote, 'the creature wants some recreation & as he is perfectly well shall have it'.[25] Cunningham Greg's other guests—'a large party formed by the Nelson Club'—were presumably all gentlemen, and their seats were in a 'Stage Box'—a pretty sophisticated company for Tom. The play was apparently some sort of a burlesque, for Matty goes on to explain that there would be lots of variety to appeal to Tom 'unless the hunted Tower has a different effect, but I have prepared him to laugh at the cheat & directed him to be sent home in a Chair'.[25]

With commendable restraint, in view of Sarah's recent protest, Dr. Drennan confined his remarks on this escapade to the following brief sentence: 'I hope Tom got no cold at the play, and that he was not too much transported in his feelings'. Subsequently we learn that 'Tom is in perfect good health & spirits in spite of bad weather. A riotous gallery the night he was at the Play spoiled his amusement, but I was glad to find did not frighten him, tho' the soldiers drew their swords'. Certainly Mrs. M'Tier need never fear that the courage, so gratifyingly displayed at the age of two [p. 12] on the occasion of the King's birthday parade, was declining. To-day we are constantly being told by those who conduct research into juvenile reactions to films etc. how difficult it is to ascertain exactly what it is that frightens children. One would have thought that a riot in a theatre, illumined only by he flickering light of many candles, following a hairraising show and resulting in drawn swords, would have been terrifying enough for the four-year-old, not to mention his being subsequently boxed up alone in a sedan chair in the dark and carried home by two strange men. But apparently, in this otherwise sensitive child, there was not the slightest sign of panic.

Within a week Tom was again at the theatre. He and his Aunt 'dined at Mr. Greg's and went to a most stupid Opera

of which we were *both* heartily tired . . . No chair cd. be got
and we walked home in Snow. Today he appears fagged and
we will not go again'.[27]

With March came the fifth birthday: 'This is Tom's
birthday, the 24th,' remarked his father rather casually in
one of his letters to Mrs. M'Tier—and there was no mention
of a present—but in the previous letter there was this spontaneous, loving message: 'Give mine & his Mother's best
kiss to our dearest Tom'.[28]

# Chapter V: Five years old

EXCEPT for the important fact that he did not go to school, that he did not even attend any of the classes held by various masters in the town, Tom was now a typical little school-boy, by turns naughty, rough, mischievous, entertaining, alluring, lazy—about lessons—and ceaselessly energetic about other things. Nevertheless, having said all that—for which there is ample proof in Mrs. M'Tier's letters —it is evident that the qualities that so endeared him to others more than held their own against this upsurge of normal, healthy spirits. In April of this sixth year, with an exurberant delight in Thomas, and in the Spring bursting forth on the dreadful monotony of the two old cousins' ceaseless pre-occupation with their ailments, his Aunt sends this vivid picture to Dublin:

> ... the everlasting theme of Aches & ailments poured into my ears from Morning 'till bedtime by both speaking of them at one time in different tones—But they do both suffer greatly & instead of feeling for each other, it is an eternal comparison & jibbing of which is worst, taking off each others pain, to add to their own. But all my old friends & favorites without are renewing their endeavours to please me, & succeed. The Black bird has taken his post, calls me to it by the most soothing melody, then pauses, to let me reflect with gratitude. My Robins never forsake me, the flowers of the Spring please my eye by appearing in their new situations placed to more advantage. My sweet Boy handles his Trowel, & asks to read the Parable of the Sower. In short this is the place I hope to live most of my allotted time in, even as it is, & not to be too sorry to bid it farewell.[1]

In the matter of education Mrs. M'Tier stuck resolutely
to her own unconventional ideas, though relatives and others
began to infer that the time had come for these unorthodox
methods to give place to more serious instruction. Close to
his fifth birthday she writes:

> *Tom reads (not much at a time) in Sandford & Merton
> & I think will read, as he does everything, agreeably. As
> for writing, counting & everything else, tho' I know I
> cow'd by this time have brought it to phrase about, I saw
> it wd. rob him of so much liberty etc. etc. I gave it quite
> up.*[2]

Cousin Young expressed the 'desire of putting him to Boyer
our best reading master' and Dr. Drennan wrote that 'the
first Master I should wish for Tom would be a French
Master and an intimacy in any House or School where it is
the only language spoken'.[3]

One evening at a small party a guest inquired of Mrs.
M'Tier about Tom. At the mention of his name Mrs. Bruce,
another guest, remarked, with some show of carelessness,
that 'Mrs. M'Tier puts him to no school but the dancing'.
This lady's husband was the Rev. Wm. Bruce, Mrs.
M'Tier's minister and, moreover, Principal of Belfast
Academy, established some twenty years earlier to provide
up-to-date education for boys, so the remark was hardly to
be taken as disinterested. Nothing daunted, Matty replied:
'Tom can read a little, write a little, count a little, ride a
little and if I can get him to read a play well [again, the
love of the theatre] 'tis all I profess.' At this recital of
accomplishments yet another guest exclaimed, 'I wish you
had my Bruce under your care, who, at the same age, can
do nothing'.[4]

Meanwhile, Dr. Drennan, charmed by the 'perspicuity of
expression and precision of ideas' of a certain Dr. Perceval,
one of his medical colleagues, wrote again to Matty that

PLATE VI: CABIN HILL,

*as it was about* 1803.

there is 'nothing I shd. more eagerly wish for my children than a calm, clear connected flow of elocution, even tho' it might often appear pedantic'[5] and, no doubt with this object in mind, he sent Tom, as a New Year's gift, 'a little book, some of which I wish him to get by heart'. Unfortunately the title is not mentioned. Possibly it was one of the small encyclopaedic volumes prepared for children and greatly in vogue at that time. One such, *The Youth's Instructor*, produced in 1802, included in its assorted contents: Moral Stories, Songs & Fables, Historical Episodes, Bible Stories, Accounts of some of the most Stupendous Works of Art, Prayers & Graces adapted to different Ages, The Story of King Lear, A description of the Pyramids, Poems by Watts, Pope and others; terminating with a dissertation on 'Tenderness towards **Brutes**'.

Whatever the book, Mrs. M'Tier replied that 'Tom will do with yr. present as you direct, for he is very proud of yr. attentions, & presses much to have all yr. letters read to him', but there is no indication that the idea of a pedantic 'flow of elocution' would be taken up. Matty goes on to say that owing to very bad wintry weather 'the exercise of his heels must be given up for a time, but when I tell you that he is reading Blair's Sermons you will not think ill of his head'. And, as if this was not sufficient vindication of her methods, she adds triumphantly 'indeed I felt proud yesterday on questioning the youngest of 5 Boys of Mr. Seeds, now at the Acy.,* to find that tho' *there* & 7 years old, he was only in Manson's Spelling Book'.[6] No question of Master Seeds being able to read Blair's sermons!

Then, as a final answer to all criticism, there arrived in Dublin a few days later, two letters from Tom himself— his first letters, written as will be seen, with exquisite care

---

* Belfast Academy.

and style, though a discerning glance can discover where the little hand grew tired. The first letter reads as follows:

> *I love your Commendation my dear Papa and your letters, so I got one of the Poems by heart you sent me, and a guinea from my good Cousin Young.*
> *I have got a little help with this, but I hope soon to do better, and not go back like T. R. Robinson.*
>                    *Your own affect. Boy*
>                                      *T.H.D.*[7]

The sheet of paper has been ruled in pencil, no doubt by 'Aunt Atier'. Thomas Romney Robinson,* a pupil at the aforementioned Belfast Academy, had, the year before, at the age of ten, published a collection of poems in order to collect the necessary funds to enable him to proceed forthwith to Trinity College, Dublin. The Robinson family was well known in Belfast, the father was an artist who had been taught by George Romney, and no doubt his precocious son was the not-too-seriously accepted model for aspiring little boys.

Tom's other letter, reproduced here [*facing p. 48*], is to his Mother. The 'little friends' were two tiny teeth. Sarah and her husband would instantly recall the delight with which they had discovered them four years earlier, perhaps they would even remember the shawl given to Betty the nursemaid to celebrate the great event. Could any mother have received a more adorable first letter? The despatch of the little teeth throws into high relief Matty's tender feeling for the child *and* his parents, and Dr. Drennan, as he read and re-read the carefully transcribed Cowper poem, would be assured that, however unusual were his sister's methods as a teacher, she was training his dearly-loved little

---

* He became a Doctor of Divinity and Astronomer at the Observatory, Armagh.

son in the tradition of unrepentant liberalism that he and
she so highly prized.

The following incident may have happened when ardent
practising for these very letters was taking place, and shows
that for Tom, at least, they were an occasion for humour as
well as sentiment. One day he was writing his 'copy', Aunt
M'Tier by his side. It is easy to picture the little figure, his
attention rivetted on the copper-plate headline, the pen
tightly gripped in a small round hand. Suddenly he looked
up, and, with one of his devastatingly disarming smiles
sweeping over his face, declared mischievously, 'If my Papa
saw us he wd. say, "Matty it is very foolish teaching that
Boy to write so soon" '[3]—a story that is evidence of an
almost adult companionship between Tom and his Aunt, as
well as of his quick imagination and love of the droll.

In pursuance of informal education the following request
was sent to Sarah:

> *In one of Tom's little Books (I believe Miss Edge-*
> *worth's) she mentioned a sort of useful toy which must be*
> *very gratifying to that natural inclination of Chiln. for*
> *building Houses—little Bricks—. I wish I cou'd get them*
> *with dissected Door frames—Windows, etc. If these were*
> *each mark'd with their particular name, & even some*
> *little Models of the different* Orders of Architecture *it wd.*
> *most easily produce in play a useful & genteel knowledge.*
> *I also wish for the different forms of square, triangle,*
> *Oval, Octagon, Hex: etc. etc. in the same way.* These *I*
> *cd. get made here, but at the Tunbridge W[are]*
> *H[ouse] perhaps they may be neater, & fitter for my*
> *purpose. If they are not there, send for them for me to*
> *England.*[9]

Another letter ends with this abrupt demand: 'Are there
not in Dublin silkworms to be sold, if so send me some. I
have kept them & know how to treat them. I want them for

Tom'.[10] Unfortunately all that came back was the laconic reply, 'No silkworms to be had'. What interesting and enterprising ideas!

Items of local interest were not forgotten, and Tom was taken to 'the Poor House to see its inhabitants, old and young, when, for his *name*, he received many blessings. [Dr. Drennan had been connected with the Poor House Infirmary before setting up practice in Dublin, and began there vaccination against smallpox.] I showed him our former house, saying it was *there* his Papa lived when he was a lad'.[12]

If Mrs. M'Tier maintained her hold on academic instruction, dancing, on the other hand, was dealt with at the highest professional level. As we have seen, Tom vastly enjoyed skipping about. During the summer his aunt had taken him to a barn dance 'not large enough to allow of anything but reels'. When the time for departure arrived Tom begged to be allowed to stay, and 'do let me dance' was repeated 'so often and so eagerly' that he was allowed to 'take out a little boy he said cd. dance & try what they two cd. do. He flew to the Boy & really astonished me with his rustic steps, straight back & unwearied zeal. With difficulty I got him away from general plaudits, which *he* joined by clapping & compleated his full satisfaction by giving the fiddler a piece of silver to the amount of 6d.'[13] So when, with approaching winter, she and Tom moved from Cabin Hill to Belfast Matty wrote that she intended 'to put Tom to a very excellent dancing Master'.[14] After a lesson or two he so much intrigued Cousin Young with 'his Dancing School bow' that she offered to pay for the classes. During the winter occasional jaunts to Cabin Hill had to be carefully planned for, wrote Matty, 'I do not chuse that he shd. miss the dancing'.

During this year Tom's general health seems to have been excellent and he was growing fast. Before leaving Dublin his height had been measured on the chimney piece, and from time to time 'a cord' arrived from Belfast indicating how much he had grown. Now, two new suits had to be purchased for him, 'he has got nothing since you saw him, & you may suppose both from the time & from the cord I sent you that he is in want of them. They are made with long sleeves and so fashionably large, that tho' they cheat one in an idea of his bulk they injure the extreme neatness of his figure'.[15] Tom had always been slight—a fact that gave rise to his father's statement that he 'could be drawn through an alderman's ring'.

The child continued to make many friends. When in Belfast he had 'the free range of this fine, safe, open street [the Parade] & D[onegall] P[lace], with an increasing acquaintance & Ld. Edward lately enlisted, but as he & Belfast* seldom get out of the bounds of their own Shrubbery, Tom & his flying course after his flying hoop are objects of envy till their poneys, servants, etc. attend on their morning ride, & then, I fear, the passion changes its residence, but 'tis only for a moment'. Again: 'No place can be more safe & delightful than this for health & improvement for as he mixes [aged five!] with a variety of people, particularly the Draipers [linen merchants who congregated at the White Linenhall facing the Parade to do business], it opens his mind & keeps up his natural frankness & freedom of address—which I wd. grieve ever to see him lose. At present he is both in mind and body all I cou'd wish, & quite a gentleman by *nature*, not instruction'.[16]

Very occasionally he wandered too far and, wrote Matty, 'I was forced to torture myself & others the other Day by whipping him for having been out from two till 5, & then not to be found. You start! but he is used to much liberty in certain bounds—every one knows him & takes care of him.

---

* Lord Belfast and Lord Edward Chichester, sons of the second Marquis of Donegall, who lived at that time in Donegall Place.

He returned like a happy innocent bird unconscious of what
I had prepared against his bottom and my own heart, but
I performed it & he was not so much the worse of it as a
pair of new Drawers'.[17] Never again, however, could she
school herself to such self-torture.

Lord Donegall's butler, Henry, was one of Tom's new
acquaintances. This man

> *frequently asks him to walk, & as he appears decent as*
> all *his* [Lord D's.] *servants are, I generally comply—*
> *glad to get him a safe guard. The other day he did not*
> *come home for his dinner till* 5. *Having repeatedly whip-*
> *ped him for this before, I only inquired where & with*
> *whom he had been. With Henry. Where did he take you?*
> *To Grimmers. What did he give you? Cake. Where did*
> *you go afterwards? To a Beer House. Well, what did you*
> *do there?* We *drank two quarts of ale. All yourselves?*
> *No, two more* joined us. *Henry call'd me* his *Son, but*
> *they did not believe him & then he said I was Dr.*
> *Drennan's. Now Wm. and even you* [this letter is to
> Sarah] *are quite frighten'd—never fear—he is not a pin*
> *the worse in my Eyes, tho' Miss B. thinks him* fallen off
> *since his last trip to Belfast. The truth is he is* not *so*
> courteous *in his manners, relishing Boys & Boyish tricks*
> *better than old women. But I must not allow him to sport*
> *them on Miss Y. who fears him* now. *He got her Snuff*
> *Box the other Day, stole it away, emptied out all the*
> *Snuff, replaced it with sand & return'd pressing her to*
> *take snuff. She suspected him & thought she escaped a*
> *dreadful mistake. For my life I cannot punish him for*
> *such things & I own talking does not now do, for his*
> *spirits are excessive & Miss B. groans in the fear of his*
> *being grown foolish.*[18]

Dr. Drennan made no comment on the prank played on
Cousin Young, and the escapade with the butler was allowed

to pass, but he returned again to his fear of Tom being
allowed to play, unsupervised, with little boys 'who are full
of dangerous tricks, and I don't think a number of them
should ever be left together without a watch over them'.
Which drew from Mrs. M'Tier the sharp rejoinder that
Tom is receiving 'all the Masculine education his Aunt can
give him, while his brother in the city with his timid
Father. . . .'|[19]

There was no need, however, for Miss Bigger to 'groan'
about the foolishness of Tom's high spirits, or to decry his
temporary fall from intellectual precocity. His wit, his quick
perception, the appreciation of situations hitherto meaning-
less, and the ability to put two and two together in more
senses than one; the wide vistas opening up before him, and
these various new acquaintances—all this led him into that
mischievousness, even wiliness which, to a greater or lesser
degree, is every child's method of testing new powers. The
world to Tom at five years old was a very exciting place.
Some months before Mrs. M'Tier had written, 'I shall be
much on my guard in what I now say before *him*, for he
listens and repeats things one wd. never think of—nor do
I wish to restrain him by the idea of impropriety'. This
observation was occasioned by an embarrassing situation
when

> *the other night in company there was much needless pity*
> *bestowed on Mr. Bristow for the loss of his Wife, he,*
> *Tom, surprised us by saying that it was no pity at all for*
> *he was a great brute. I called on him for an explanation of*
> *such an assertion, he stuck to his text repeating he* was *a*
> Great Brute *& that it was She was to be* pit'd. *Worse &*
> *worse. I called on him for his authority—he gave his*
> *Aunt Ann, but by saying 'Mrs. B. had lost her little Son*
> *& bedfellow' the matter was softened into truth.*[20]

Soon after old Mrs. Drennan's death he inquired if his
Grandmother had made a will. ' "Yes," I replied, and with

a mixed smile he added, "She did not leave me anything." '21

But nothing, nothing at all, destroyed his loveableness,
his gaiety and his genius for making adequate response to a
new situation. As if to illustrate this, but actually as a matter
of course, Mrs. M'Tier relates that she had recently given
two successive parties:

> *in both he appeared the young Master of the House. He
> found Tom Sinclaire* [an older boy] *the only unemploy'd
> gentleman & attached himself to him, gave him his
> Mama's first Pocket Book, which contained matter quite
> suited to Sinclaire for above an hour. Tom then intro-
> duced a small Table with his Maps, this also suited his
> companion & I question if he has been paid such attention
> to or been so well entertained for these 7 years.*

But that was not all: the great Mr. Greg, one of the richest
and most influential of Belfast's merchants, then entered—

> *...who seldom plays cards. Tom, entirely of himself,
> ask'd him if he wd. play backgammon, & to the great
> entertainm't of the Company, the good natured man
> accepted Tom's invitation & really play'd about the Men
> with him.*22

Always that superb gift, astonishing in a five-year-old, of
laying himself out to entertain—to give pleasure, but without the slightest suggestion of 'showing-off' or of attracting
attention to himself.

It is fascinating to speculate as to what he must have
looked like at this elderly card-party: perhaps the silhou-
ette, or 'shade' as Mrs. M'Tier called it, was taken at just
this time [*frontispiece*]. The long drain-pipe trousers were
probably made of buff coloured fustian; the full-skirted
jacket may have been a lovely sapphire blue or perhaps olive

green; and the little white ruff, carefully starched and laundered—uncomfortable no doubt, but willingly accepted as a necessary accessory for a great occasion—heightened the healthy colour of his face. Notice how carefully the tousled head has been brushed and groomed.

Dancing continued to be Tom's delight and 'if practice is necessary he takes it abundantly for he cross's the Room in steps & they send for him to Mr. Dobbs & Sinclaires to help out the country dance set in the private school'.[22]

During the Spring of that year there occurred one of those intermittent outbreaks of fever which, with greater or less severity struck Ireland with horrifying frequency, and which after the Famine of 1845-48 exacted such a devastating toll. Mrs. M'Tier planned to take Thomas to the fresh country air of Cabin Hill and wrote to her brother for advice. In all his professional work Dr. Drennan was an ardent advocate of scrupulous cleanliness, and his reply enunciates the now generally accepted theory that this fever was the result of malnutrition and unhygienic conditions. For these reasons it rarely penetrated the homes of the well-to-do, except in such cases, and there were many of them, when the well-to-do had direct contact with the sufferers by distributing food and comforts. He writes:

*With respect to Tom's going out to the Country, I have no fear of Fever if he is kept at a distance from it, much less than a field, for it might be in the next house, if there was a certainty of having no communications with any of its inhabitants. One should therefore be always cautious of letting Tom go into any of the adjoining cabins or staying in them, or of playing with children of dirty cloathing, particularly where fever is, or has been some time before, and the precaution shd. be taken that the Servants at Cabin Hill for their own sakes, do not go into such cabins, or sit down on the beds in them, for they often are the carriers of infection into genteel families. But with the cleanliness, frequent changes of dress, and the heavenly blessing of pure water outside & in, there is not much room for apprehension of the worst fever, at a few yards distance. I think if you cannot answer for a proper seclusion of all the family from the House where there is Fever, it would be improper to let Tom go out, particularly if his playfellows belong to the House, and they come much and closely together. It is the want of changes of cloathing and bedding which keeps the fever so long in these cabins, and the inhabitants may have got quite well, and yet others staying long in such places, & particularly lying on their beds, may get the infection. But keep your distance and you are quite safe, nor is this low cabin fever apt to come into clean kept houses, & therefore with precaution I see little to fear.*[23]

There seems to have been no widespread epidemic in the Cabin Hill locality and soon Mrs. M'Tier made several suggestions that Tom should go to Dublin for 'a month or two', or better still, that William should come north accompanied by his father, as she 'really did not like that Tom shd. be wean'd from his Parents, or they from him'. William arrived in June to stay, as before, with Aunt Ann. Memories of the militant reactions that assailed both boys on the previous visit being fresh in Dr. Drennan's mind, he warned his sister: 'I hope the brothers will get better acquainted without any jealousy arising between them, particularly in Tom's mind, which you shd. be watchful about, and make them have a mutual respect to each other and generally have one in town & one in the country to sharpen their affection and appetite for each other's company'. To Tom he writes a long letter on the subject:

No formal opening.

*It is a long time since I wrote to my dear boy, but both your Mother and I have thought very often about you, and although we did not see you we were well pleased to hear by your Aunt that you continued to be a very good boy, that you had learned to read and could spell pretty well, which you must do very well before you are taught to write.* [This was written before Tom's letters to his parents.] *When you are able to read what I write to you and to answer me by writing yourself, I shall send you letters very often. Your Mama and I have agreed to send your brother William on a visit to his Aunt Ann, and I hope my dear Tom you will be glad to see him, not only because he is your brother but because he loves you, and often speaks of you. Therefore you will love one another, and be kind to him because you are the eldest. He will show you all his books and toys, and in return, when the fruit is ripe you will take him into the garden, when Cousin Young allows you, to eat gooseberries, if they be ripe. He often has talked of sitting with his good Cousin Young on the bed while she gave him some of her fruit, and I hope she will be able as soon as the fruit is ripe to sit in the garden while you and your brother Willy are busy gathering the best gooseberries to lay in her lap, for she has been very kind to you in allowing you to remain at Cabin-Hill so long, and to get into better health and spirits than you had in Dublin. William takes down with him a nice plumb cake which his Mama desires him to share with his aunts and cousins, and with you, and then to get a little bit to himself, and he also takes some red herrings which your aunt M'Tier wrote us to send. If it be in my power I shall see you myself before the end of the year, and bring you and William some pretty present from Dublin. Your brother William has a very good memory, tho' he is not yet able to read, but he can tell the little stories in his own picture books almost as well as if he read them. But you will help him to read and you will be kind to him, and love him, and I am sure he will love you, and it is to make you love each other as dear brothers that I have sent him to Belfast for a month or two, so that I expect never to hear of any such thing as a quarrel between you because you are brothers. You have got another little brother since you left Dublin whose name is Lennox. He is a fine child. He was inoculated for the cow-pock and has passed over the complaint very well. Your Mama desires her dear love and duty to them all and tell Aunt M'Tier to write for you an answer to this letter, as soon as she receives it, and to tell us how Wm. got down.*

*Tell Cousin Young that nothing could do more good than adding Soap to her other bounty of clean linen to the poor people who had the Fever near Cabin-Hill. With soap and pure water properly apply'd there would scarcely be such a thing heard of as Fevers among the poor, which are almost always owing to or at least kept up by, the want of using properly what is at their doors. Cleanliness is the virtue of the Body as Virtue is the cleanliness and purity of the mind, and if you keep this truth in your head and in your heart, you will become a good man and a pleasing gentleman.*

*When you see Margaret M'Tier give her our love, thank her from me for the kind present she intends for my use and give my very respectful compliments to her Aunts. Tell your Cousin Ann Jane that her nephew Lennox dined with us yesterday, and played a rubber of whist with Mrs. Cunningham & your Mama in the evening, and that he appears in very good health and spirits. And now, dear Tom, let me repeat to you to be always kind and attentive to little William, and when you play together and eat gooseberries, and are very happy, then think of your Papa and Mama who love you both so well, and will always love you, if you love one another, and learn to read well, and spell well, and write well, and be*

*civil, obliging and attentive to every one around you—*
*for if you are not good boys, you will never become good*
*men. God bless you my dear Tom, and believe me your*
*affectionate father.*

*W. Drennan.*[25]

Prosy and overdone to us—but the child to whom this
epistle was addressed received it with an up-rising of pride
and love. Mrs. M'Tier reports that 'Tom's sweet little Eyes
twinkled with the tear of sensibility & proud pleasure over
yr. letter to him',[26] and the meeting of the brothers at Cabin
Hill, two days after William's arrival in Belfast, exceeded,
in its felicity, all expectations. Matty wrote to Sarah:

*I feel I would not be acting by the golden rule if I was*
*to delay writing any longer, at a time too when there is*
*a double claim upon me, possessed of the half of yr.*
*domestic happiness. Miss Y. sent in the Car on Monday*
*for my Sister & Wm. . . . Tom and he met with much*
*pleasure, & as the former is the head taller, & had on it*
*a rustic cap also* sleeves *to his coat, Willy stole many a*
*sly look at him. He knew every one & every place, and*
*was so animated & taken up with Tom, Drum, Gun, etc.*
*that we in the parlor got little good of him, nothing cd.*
*be fonder & more agreeable than the two brothers, and*
*were sorry to part, which at* that *time we thought best,*
*Miss Y. was poorly & the additional noise might not*
*have been agreeable . . . He produced, &* left *here, his*
*nice Plumb Cake on the tea table in the small circle of all*
*his northern relations. He is, I think, very little altered,*
*a fine, frank bold spirited manly, handsome boy . . . He*
*appears to think rather too much of his power with a* stick
*& delights to drive all before him with it . . . Certainly*
*these two boys have* not an idea *of shame — take care of*
*your daughter* [an oblique reference to yet another
pregnancy].[27]

When haymaking commenced William was sent for to
Cabin Hill, 'and has been with us ever since, well, fond &
happy. Tom looks like a Creole beside him and seems to
*feel* the difference. A little jealousy of affection still lurks
there, but', says Matty with her usual wisdom, 'it will wear
away better by not being much noticed. Wm. is clear of this
& so fond of Tom & being like him, that if he breaks his
neck the other will do it also. I took them', she adds, 'to
Meeting in Belfast on Sunday'.[28] One wishes that Hugh
Thompson could have drawn that little party. Mrs. M'Tier,
formidable in her Sabbath attire, seated in the high backed
pew, flanked on either side by a seraphic nephew, one a
'blooming rustic' scrubbed into Sabbath neatness, the other
still somewhat awed by strange surroundings.

All emotional difficulties quickly disappeared and for the
two brothers there was nothing but happiness in the long
summer days at Cabin Hill 'hourly gormandising of fruit'.
Then in August Dr. Drennnan, his wife, baby Lennox and
his nurse, all arrived on a visit to the north. They stayed for
a fortnight and it must have been a joyful time. There are
no details of what they did, except that Mrs. M'Tier dis-
carded her mourning—it was now nine months since her
mother, old Mrs. Drennan, had died—and doubtless there
were parties, and many friends to be introduced to this
charming sister-in-law. As always, Matty seems to have been
much attracted by Sarah: when writing to her brother on
hearing of their safe return to Dublin she says, 'It is pleasant
to arrive in sunshine to a clean house [painters and decora-
tors had been busy] & with a companion that wd. gild any
scene. While she is spared to you, and her health preserved,
you ought never to feel unhappy'[29]; and again she refers to
Sarah as 'the grand hinge' on which the welfare and comfort
of the whole family depended. William returned home with
his parents, and it was a very sad parting for Tom. He
'dropped in spirits from the day you went away, eat little,

went to bed after Dinner, did not wish to play, & his own acct. was, that he was neither well nor ill [an excellent description of misery] ... He told Miss Young no one kissed him at parting but Willy & indeed he put both his arms about his waist very fast'.[29] Tom was still terribly sensitive to either grief or joy.

It was at this psychological moment that the long-promised pony appeared. History does not relate any spectacular results accruing from lottery tickets, but there is definite mention of three solid golden guineas being provided by good Cousin Young. Dr. Drennan hopes that the pony and 'camomile tea every morning' together with the fresh juice of vegetables such as 'robin-run-i'-the-hedge sweetened with honey or a tablespoonful of malt'[30] will improve Tom's appetite. Grizzle, the pony, was a great success—'Tom never better, mad with spirits. He is now mounted on the Poney & gone to Greenville to join the children there on an Ass. His riding is wonderful ... he is equipped with a new briddle & Whip, but the Goat's Skin is yet wanting to cover the pad made for him'.[31]

The happy family gathering at Cabin Hill had brought Tom much nearer to his parents. Ever since that first morning in Belfast, three years ago, when he had wakened in a strange room to see his father's portrait hanging on the wall before him, that father had been his constant, if rather distant mentor, and this relationship had been greatly strengthened by Dr. Drennan's visit to Cabin Hill a year later, and during Tom's stay in Dublin. But now, since that joyful time at Cabin Hill, with his parents, William and dear Aunt 'Atier' all there together on his own familiar, secure territory, his father and mother had become objects of real love and affection. Again and again Matty reminds her brother of this—'He heard yr. last letter read out & observed *his* name was never once in it, a circumstance he will not soon forget'.[32] 'Tom is coming on very fast in his reading, he

desires me to tell you *this*, for he loves praise dearly.'[33]
'Tom is very proud of yr. attentions & presses much to have
all yr. letters read to him.' And yet again—'Tom is in high
spirits & a complete rattle, he is just now climbing beside me
shouting, "up I go, Neck or nothing as the *Prophet* says,"
& he desires me to tell his Mama to write'.[34]

In the autumn he and his aunt went back to Belfast and
lessons were resumed. The gaiety of his nature could bear no
sadness and we hear that 'Tom has just now been obliged to
quit the history of Joseph in tears, & as our novel heroes
frequently you know declare they must die, we are obliged
to make him leave the room in all scenes of delicate dis-
tress,'[35] which may, or may not, have been a slight overstatement on the part of Mrs. M'Tier. However, 'as he flies
tragedy he loves comedy & made a most wonderful natural
attempt at reading one, to his cousin's astonishment, the
other night. Have you any farces? Send one or two down'.[36]
An assortment was despatched by return for 'dear Tom'.

Christmas that year was spent at Cabin Hill—one of the
few times that the festival is mentioned in this correspondence, but it must be admitted that there is no great evidence
of jollification, Mrs. M'Tier commenting that 'a merry one
is seldom obtained at my time of life, when it [the festive
season] is only a memorandum of departed friends'.[37] One
hopes that there was some cheery entertainment for Tom.
The weather was atrocious, too severe for much riding on
Grizzle, everyone had colds, and very soon Mrs. M'Tier
was writing to Dublin that 'Tom's cold has turn'd to so
severe a cough, particularly at night, that there is much
reason to believe it a chin cough, got, about three weeks ago
from a girl who appeared to have it, coming in to the seat
with him at Meeting & thus baffling all my care'. In order
to confirm this diagnosis before writing, Mrs. M'Tier had
'gone to town yesterday & call'd on Mrs. Seeds, whose
children are all lately recovered from it. To my observing

he did not *hoop*, she reply'd they wd. be weeks without doing so, & some never did'. Mrs. Seeds said that Tom should be kept from additional cold and frosty air, and, if Dr. Drennan approved, that he should be rubbed 'with something of which I forget the name—I think like Ambrosia— several bottles of which Mrs. Seeds had got from Dub: and found the greatest use'. Meantime, Tom had been given a mixture of treacle and vinegar & 'at bed time 5 drops of Laudm.' and then put on a diet of 'essence of Malt, Light food—mostly fruit & grapes, both night & Day'.[38]

Dr. Drennan replied with some professional scorn for these amateur opinions:

*I received your Letter—I should rather think it is not the whooping cough which has attacked Tom. I shall say shortly what I think best to be try'd immediately. I would have him get every night at bed-time two tea spoonfulls of a bottle in which two grains of emetic tartar are dissolved in two ounces of Ipocacoanha Wine. It is designed to make him sick and throw up once or twice, but not more. After one or two nights perhaps at first it will have that effect. If it has not you may give him a teaspoonful in the morning. I would rub his breast night & morning with what is called volatile oil, Hartshorn and oil shaken together with the quantity of a drachm of Laudanum added to it. The linament should be so smart as to inflame the skin a little and let it be covered afterwards with thin flannel, it should be shaken before use, and rubbed gently with a soft hand. This is all I advise at present, for your diet and regimen seem very proper, whatever the complaint may turn out. I consider Cabin Hill as a damp place particularly at this season, and whether the removal into town for a few days would tend to increase the cough by going, or check it by change of air & a dryer air, you will be the best judge.[39]*

Mrs. M'Tier answered, somewhat sharply, that Tom was in excellent spirits, that she had got the ointment made up and the Ipecacuanha Wine, but that she had little doubt that it *was* the 'hooping Cough'. As for the slighting remarks about Cabin Hill—'no situation can be better than C: H: which instead of damp is the dryest House about the Country, & Mud Walls are more so than any when properly preserved'.[40]

From a hundred-odd miles away Dr. Drennan continued to pooh-pooh the idea of whooping cough. 'I have little doubt,' he wrote in a few days, 'it is merely in consequence of a cold caught at the Meeting House wh. of all places is, I think, in winter most unfit for children, there being, I believe no fire or stove in your Belfast House from its first erection, and sitting in this cold bath of damp, for two hours, without moving, and coming out afterwards, perhaps exposed to a severe winter wind, must give coughs, if anything can. . . . I think,' he continues, 'any old woman in the parish might have determined in this time, from the very sound of the Cough whether it be of the Chincough kind or not.'[41]

Eventually the verdict of whooping cough was accepted, though the attack was so slight 'that he is likely to get over this unpleasant disorder wihout the loss of anything but his Dancing, which is all he regrets . . . He will bloom in the Spring & be able to venture to a Meeting House without a Stove'.[42]

If the severe weather had shortened tempers, it had also increased the infirmity of Cousin Young. She could no longer walk and a chair had been adapted for her use, 'it moves on Castors & one of the things Tom is proudest of is helping to Wheel her into the Parlor'.

Thoroughly bored by 'a close confinemt. for above a month' [because of whooping cough], Matty determined to move into Belfast 'to try the Town air & share a little in its amusements'. Tom came with her and they went to the Play

House, 'where he was in raptures with the Forty Thieves'.[43]
But in a few days 'having got a mask, with which he proposed much entertainment in the Country', she allowed him
to go back to Cabin Hill. 'So I have been at the Parade quite
alone for above a week & intend to remain if I can another
Month, but not without him, for whom I sent today.'[44] Even
yet, she could not 'want' the child. Poor little Tom: 'He
knew it did not please me,' she wrote a few days later 'his
going off to C.H. the last time, & the Servant discovering
him in tears in his own room, he told her it was because his
Aunt M. wd. be alone on Sunday'.[45] A slight incident, but
what a vivid picture. The mask had instantly raised all
Tom's imagination, his delight in the comic, his wild
enthusiasm for fun, for the jokes that could be played on the
Cabin Hill servants, and on the neighbouring cottagers. Such
endless possibilities resulted in insistent demands to get back
to the country. Then in the midst of the hilarity and excitement his tender little heart remembered Aunt M'Tier—all
by herself on a Sunday, and he knew how she hated to be
alone. If ever a child answered up to all that is implied in
that difficult, yet distinctive, eighteenth century word 'sensibility', surely it was Tom.

Sarah was expecting her sixth child, or rather as Dr.
Drennan wrote she, 'threatens me with twins, but I believe
there is no reason to fear'. Perhaps preoccupation with this
unacceptable possibility accounted for the seemingly churlish
attitude towards the whooping cough episode. Matty was
already suggesting that William should come again to Cabin
Hill to be out of the way. Tom's sixth birthday was in sight.
No record remains of any celebrations, but this cryptic postscript on a letter dated March 1st, from Matty to her
brother: 'let me know Tom's B.D. & do it this week',
indicates that she did not intend to let the occasion pass
unnoticed, strange though it is that the date was not already
fixed in her memory.

# Chapter VI: The seventh year

TOM'S seventh year began uneventfully enough. 'His gentility of person continues', but so also did his school-boyish behaviour, and his Aunt had reluctantly, if indulgently, to report that 'his manners do not improve, he is become very mischievous when I am not present, & there have been secret friendly hints given me of his affecting the blackguard. But don't be serious about this, though I was in my reprimand, 'tis nothing but an affectation boys fall into'.[1]

Sarah's twins did not materialise, and the birth of a little daughter called for this realistic comment from Mrs. M'Tier to her brother:

> *Your* annual *and immediate intelligence demands its usual congratulation, & you may bestow it where most justly due. The subject in no light gives* Tom *pleasure, and for a Sister he has a decided prejudice, which I hope will one Day be improved into a merited partiality for a fair Sally. He desire his love to his Mother.*[1]

A pang of conscience, however, produced a few days later this additional message:

> *Sarah will think I might have adressed* her *more particularly than a tack of love, but really getting children are such common events I had nothing to say upon the subject.*[2]

Arrangements for William's visit were still under consideration when the death of Cousin Young made it necessary for Dr. Drennan to hasten to Belfast, and he brought his second son with him. Though the journey was made with all speed they were late for the old lady's funeral, which took place at 6 a.m. on the day they arrived. However, arrangements were immediately made for Tom and

William to have black suits, and for the servants to have suitable mourning.[3]

Cousin Young's death initiated important developments in the Drennan circle. Mrs. M'Tier rejoiced in the bequest of Cabin Hill, while the greater part of the old lady's comfortable fortune was left to Dr. Drennan. With such comparative affluence it was possible for him to consider retiring from practice. He returned to Dublin, leaving William at Cabin Hill, and quickly decided to bring his family to settle in Belfast.[4] The letters of the next few months are largely concerned with legal matters and arrangements for the move.

Any superficial jealousy between the brothers had long since disappeared, and during that spring and early summer Mrs. M'Tier punctuates her epistles about the price of houses and lawyers' queries, with brief reports on two very happy, healthy little boys. On one occasion an English brother-in-law of Sarah's, while on a visit to Belfast, called at Cabin Hill. All had been prepared against his arrival in the evening but unfortunately he came instead, and quite unheralded, in the afternoon, '& seldom have I been more mortify'd than on the entrance of yr. Boys to an English Uncle. They were to be in company in the Evening & ordered not to be *dressed* till then, but potatoes wd. have grown on their hands & faces, & their very cloathes were torn to pieces. Sensible of this Tom, who generally enters with a Dash, sneak'd in like a taylor. You will say "Why is this?" It really is not in my power to help it for they roll & nestle in the sand & turf mould, just as Hens do, &, for the pleasure of building *in Mud*, forsake the meadow & Hay Cock. A pretty acct. this Uncle will take of them & their Irish Aunt to their English friends. Willy indeed told him he cd. read Holland's exercises, but Tom cd. not utter a word'.[5] Poor Tom — this is the only recorded instance when he failed to rise to the occasion.

In the middle of summer the exodus from Dublin took
place, the family eventually settling in a commodious residence behind the White Linenhall, in the recently developed
Donegall Square South. Thomas and William joined their
parents, and the correspondence between Mrs. M'Tier at
Cabin Hill and her brother in town, dwindles to intermittent
notes, mostly from Dr. Drennan and generally about matters
connected with family property. In one of these he mentions
that 'Tom was taken up yesterday in writing a Note to his
dear Aunt M'Tier, but he must be practised a little more at
the pen—both he & Wm. read & spell very tolerably'.[6]
From the following undated letter from 'dear Aunt M'Tier'
to Tom, occasioned by some unspecified ailment, we can infer
that Tom and William spent a lot of time at the country
cottage, and indeed it would seem that Dr. Drennan was,
at the moment of her writing, staying there himself:

*Dear Tom,*

*There is so little here you can relish that I eke out a
handful of Asparagus with a bowl of vulgarity for you,
& a Bouquet for yr. Mama. The first she will think odd,
but little Boys, like Breeding Ladies have whims. You
have every care & comfort & therefore ought not be to
impatient under confinement necessary to recovery, the
want of which before added much to both it & yr. disorder. You seem to like getting a note, & I shall send
one every day, answer it when you have time & ease. To
write a note at once, with freedom & tolerable correct-
ness is what I wish much you shd. attain, & to do so
practice is the only thing, & now a good opportunity. Try
to be certain as to yr. spelling, date your note, the rest I
am sure will come, of course, with the wish to please.
Your selection of an Inscription for the Moss-house was
very appropriate. I thought of one that might perhaps at
some moment be of use, when I cannot, but Dan has*

*bungled the building so, I think I will last longer. It will do for your Papa to smile at, perhaps improve—*

For
The young Drennans
while
They revere Truth
Detest everything mean, or selfish
and
Are cemented in the sweet ties
Of mutual affection.
Such only
Must remain here.

*Ask Willy (who is a critick you know) his opinion of this or yr. Papa to shorten, write properly out, etc. etc. & I will send you a little board which will do for the inscription, painted black, & the letters white. You must have it done very neatly & ready to bring out when it is proper for you to come. This weather wou'd be quite unfavorable. Yesterday was so severely cold that it prevented me asking out the children,* which at present might be a relief both to you & yr. Mama. Tell her, if so, she wd. get them out I am sure for a word to Miss G[reg], when she sees her at Mr. Bristow's. Yr. Father will write now.*
M.M.[7]

*Master Drennan,*
*Donegall Square.*

If Matty ever wrote the promised 'notes' they have not survived. A Moss-house was the period name of a garden shelter or summer-house, built in the rustic fashion at that time so greatly in vogue. Dr. Drennan's beloved Cowper had already penned an *Inscription for a Moss-house in the*

---

* Lennox and Sally.

*Shrubbery at Weston,* and though the little erection going
up in the Cabin Hill garden was intended for no stylish
purpose, but primarily as a play place for nephews, nevertheless it must have its 'very neatly' painted inscription, in
the best classical tradition.

The Drennans had barely settled into their Belfast home
when another family separation took place, caused, this time,
by a visit to the English grandparents in Shropshire. Little
Lennox and the baby Sally were left in the care of Mrs.
M'Tier while Dr. Drennan and his wife, with Thomas and
William, set off on the 13th August, 1809. In a long letter
to his sister, written on their safe arrival at Liverpool, Dr.
Drennan gives a graphic description of an eventful crossing
from Belfast, which occupied six days, and which, to the
eight-year-old Tom, must have been an unforgettable experience. After being becalmed in Belfast Lough for three days
a strong wind arose which drove the ship at speed across the
Irish Sea and on to a sandbank at the mouth of the Mersey.
They got off

> *by a rise in the tide & a good deal of Seamanship dis-*
> *played by our Captain and the Pilot, who was exceedingly*
> *surprised by the business. The boys were in bed & slept*
> *thro' the whole. Sarah & I were on deck* [this detail
> should be noted], *& it was best we were, as we knew the*
> *whole extent of the danger, which tho' not great, was*
> *alarming in the fresh Gale that blew & in such a crew*
> *of savages.*
>
> *Reaching Liverpool at 11 p.m. on a very dark night the*
> *next difficulty was where to go. We agreed that Sarah &*
> *the boys, with Felix* [a servant] *should go into the town*
> *in search of a Porter or two, and to look for a Hotel, while*
> *I staid as a guard on the Luggage. The Ship had gone off*
> *into Dock. I did stay, and after more than half an hour*
> *walking up and down in a dark night without knowing*

*where I was, I became very uneasy when two men came up & challenged me what I did there, which I told them the reason of. Notwithstanding they were the watchmen at the pier I got them to carry our luggage to the Hotel, where I found Sarah & the boys with Felix who had lost their way & this was the reason of the delay. We could not get a bed, and were obliged to hunt about & about, till we got one at last about one in the morning.*[8]

After a good sleep and an excellent breakfast of 'bread, cream & coffee' they set off 'in a coach for brother-in-law Boult's'—the English uncle who had taken the Cabin Hill household unawares—where they stayed for a week. Mr. and Mrs. Boult had 'two fine children' with whom, and with other Liverpool cousins, the Drennan boys quickly made friends. Dr. Drennan and his brother-in-law 'rambled about' the rapidly growing city, 'which,' he declared, 'I like much,' while Sarah 'was agreeably employed with affectionate relations. I spent a great part of the time with the distinguished men of the Place and the mornings either at the Lyceum or Athenaeum, two very elegant buildings combining the advantages of News-room and Library'. Among the gentlemen of 'high literary reputation' who called upon this visitor from Ireland was William Roscoe, the noted art collector and M.P. for Liverpool,* whose staunch advocacy of the abolition of slavery would, alone, have constituted a bond of friendship between them. Dr. Drennan described him as

*a man whose appearance and manner are extremely impressive. He is a favourite child of Merit and good fortune, and has risen to deserved distinction among his*

---

* Some of his Italian Primitives, now belonging to the Walker Art Gallery Liverpool, were exhibited in 1960 at the Royal Academy's exhibition *Italian, Art and Britain.*

*fellow citizens as a man of great personal worth; and in
his country, as a Man of Letters, poetical taste and various
polite erudition. We dined at his Country House at Aller-
ton with a large yet select company; where he has
collected many curiosities, a great number of pictures all
originals of the first Italian Artists, and several fine busts,
striking likenesses of the first men of the day; where he
retires from his business as a Banker to his excellent
Library and to his large Family of nine children, several
of them fine handsome accomplished young men, and
where his Father once served as a Butler to a widow Lady
of great fortune from whose Executors the Son purchased
this noble residence, and fills it with such dignity and high
hospitality. In the late procession of his friends at his
election, he took care that they should pass by a small
house built by his Father in one of the retired streets of
Liverpool.*[9]

Another dinner party in honour of the visitor was given
by a Dr. Crompton at his country house. Tom and William
—aged eight and seven—were invited and the list of notable
guests included Mr. Roscoe and Mr. Smith, 'a tutor to the
young Sheridan'.[9]

In view of the Victorian tendency to keep children stowed
away in nurseries it is most interesting how, in this Georgian
family, Tom and William were constantly with their parents
and accustomed to take their place in adult society. Not that
one imagines for a moment that they dominated the scene,
Mrs. M'Tier's notions of 'propriety' made it quite clear that
there were very definite rules which had to be observed. But
within these limits the Drennan boys had full freedom—
and enviable opportunities of meeting people, of listening
to excellent conversation and sharing in the varying experiences of a leisured and cultured society.

This eighteenth century characteristic is mentioned by

Ann Taylor* when describing her own childhood at
Lavenham in Suffolk:

> *Nurseries at Lavenham, and at that time of the day, I do*
> *not remember. The parlour and the best parlour were all*
> *that were known besides the Kitchens, and thus parents*
> *and children formed happily but one circle . . . My father*
> *and Mother were soon noted as good managers of their*
> *children; for little as either of them had experienced of*
> *a wise education, they had formed a singularly strong*
> *resolve to train their young ones with the best judgement*
> *they could exercise, and not to suffer* humoured *children*
> *to disturb either themselves or their Friends. There is*
> *scarcely an expression so fraught to my earliest recollection*
> *with ideas of disgrace and misery as that of a 'humoured*
> *child', and I should have felt truly ashamed to exhibit one*
> *of my own at my father's table.*[10]

It would appear that the Georgian child was given a far
more noticeable place in family life than was accorded to
the offspring of Victorian parents.

One wonders if, at any of these gatherings, Dr. Drennan
met Mr. John Gladstone, a rising Dissenting merchant who
had come in his youth to Liverpool from Leith in Scotland,
and whose son William Ewart was to be born within four
months of the date of these festivities.

No doubt Tom enjoyed immensely his share in all this
gaiety. Ever interested in strangers and in new situations,
his receptive nature would assimilate much of what he saw,
and much of the stimulating conversation he heard. He was
experiencing, in fact, an educative process after Mrs.
M'Tier's own heart, and we may be sure that with his
charming manners and intelligent questions he more than

---

* Her poem 'My Mother' was admired by Dr. Drennnan.

lived down that first embarrassing meeting with Uncle Boult.
Dr. Drennan mentions that Tom has already begun his
Journal and also a letter to his Aunt, neither of which, to our
sorrow, has survived.

From Liverpool the party proceeded to Chester

> *after a pretty tedious journey across the Mersey, then
> very rough, in a small boat with* 14 *people, and the rest
> of the way in an excellent carriage, with decent driver &
> fine road, worth the travelling expenses. We arrived at
> Mrs. Nicholl's House* [a sister of Sarah's], *who has a
> boarding-school of* 40 *girls, in a House that any noble
> man might occupy . . . with every accommodation of
> garden, fine walks & plantation . . . On Sunday, after
> hearing an excellent Sermon from the dissenting pastor
> who has but* £140 *per ann. with no bounty,* we went to
> the Cathedral, a most sublime ancient building and the
> first of nine churches, where we heard the Service chanted
> in full grandeur of voices, and vestments & noble organ,
> which delighted Tom exceedingly, and almost persuaded
> him to become a Papist of the Church of England . . . The
> Boys were highly diverted with the curious construction
> of the Town—the Rows, and the walk upon the Walls,
> which indeed is highly grand and picturesque.*[11]

There were two other families of relations in Chester and
after spending some days in this pleasant company the
Drennans set off on the last thirty miles of their journey to
Wem, 'where in a patriarchial spot we have met with a
parental reception from Mr. & Mrs. S'.[11] The rural attractions that awaited the travellers differed widely from the
commercial environment at Liverpool and the scholarly
atmosphere of Chester, but the Shropshire household shared

---

* A reference to the Regium Donum.

the same intellectual independence that had charmed Dr. Drennan in the other places. Old Mr. Swanwick's farm covered almost one hundred acres, and over its fields and ditches, and through its coppices, roamed the two young Irish lads in the company of still more Swanwick cousins. 'Tom is in high spirits,' writes his father shortly after their arrival, 'and busy at his journal before he takes his ride on the Donkey'.[12]

Dr. Drennan had intended that this visit should occupy only a few weeks, but it soon became evident that Sarah would not be able to face the hazards of another voyage, especially, as her husband wrote, 'while the year is swinging on one of its hinges'—an apt allusion to the autumn equinox. It was decided, therefore, to spend the winter in England and, in October, less than two months after that eventful crossing to Liverpool, Sarah gave birth to her fifth son, to be named appropriately John Swanwick. Indeed, so unprepared was she for his coming in such circumstances that it was necessary to write hastily to Matty, requesting her to send off immediately a supply of baby clothes; bundles of these would be found 'in the old mahogany chest in our room. Betty could meet you in town and get a man to pick the lock'.[13] Soon afterwards the Drennans moved from Wem to a furnished house in Chester where, with the relations nearby, life took on a settled routine.

*The boys and I sleep in one room, and rise exactly at eight, taking from my hand their glass-full of camomile tea, and breakfasting on bread and milk. The breakfast is at 9 the dinner at 2, the tea at ½ after 5, and the supper before 9. We are seldom out of bed longer than 11. The boys are with me constantly from 10 untill 12, and are not a little improved in spelling, English Grammer, the rudiments of arithmetic and of Geography. We design sending them for a quarter to a Mr. Perry who is coming*

*to settle in Chester, with a very good character, and what
they have already learn'd with me & are still to learn,
will give them an advantage at School. Willy is best at
spelling, and arithmetic, Tom at Grammer, and
Geography. He has been several days writing a long letter
to you, so long indeed that I fear it must wait for a private
hand to carry it. I wish him to write something daily, by
himself, in order to give him a stile, but as yet he appears
dis-inclined to it. We have inoculated little John for the
Cowpock, but are yet uncertain whether he has taken it ...
We have had generally some of the families from Liverpool or Shrewsbury* [more relations] *staying at this house,
and find no want of company.*[14]

Dr. Drennan wrote this letter just after Christmas when
there had been a family gathering 'of forty-three relations,
including twenty grandchildren of which number Tom was,
I believe, the eldest, and our little John the youngest. The
different branches of our Genealogical Tree are pretty well
loaded with fruit & I never saw a more affectionate and
united Family'.[14] A very happy environment for Tom.

His ninth birthday passed unnoticed, though within a
week or so of it Dr. Drennan tells his sister that the boys
'go regularly to school at 8 in the morning and to bed at
8 in the evening ... Both seem to like reading of the agreeable kind, which will I hope create a habit at least of
attending to books of instruction in some time. Tom appears
delighted with Don Quixote, & Wm. spent four shillings of
his own money on a book of entertainment yesterday. He
was run over by a Man in Drink in the Rows a night or two
ago, and his Face severely bruised, but is now as well as
ever'.[15] Considering previous references to danger, Dr.
Drennan took this incident very calmly.

Among the friends in the Chester neighbourhood was
Miss Eliza Lawrence, the successful mistress of a boarding

school for girls at Gateacre. Having at one time refused to
become the wife of Mrs. Barbauld's nephew, Arthur Aiken,
she was now about to marry Dr. Drennan's friend, Robert
Holmes, whose first wife had been a sister of Robert Emmet
—another instance of the strong connection between the
Irish liberals and the dissenter radicals of the north of
England.[16]

Having got his family comfortably settled, Dr. Drennan
made a hurried visit to Belfast to attend to legal affairs and
to the letting of his house, and no doubt, to encounter a
bombardment of questions from Mrs. M'Tier regarding
Tom's welfare and his educational progress. He returned to
Chester armed with gifts, that to Tom being a watch, for
we read: 'How delighted Tom and William have been
with your presents . . . I have since dinner left Tom mar-
shalling eight of his cousins with his brother at their head,
and giving them the word of command, with his watch on
his Fob & with as military an air as the times require'.[17]

It is curious that during this English sojourn, which
lasted from August 1809 till the following May, very few
letters from Mrs. M'Tier have been preserved. During all
that time she had charge of Lennox and little Sally, and
was also responsible for finding and installing a tenant in
her brother's house in Belfast, to mention two major topics
of mutual interest. So, when one recalls the ceaseless flow of
letters that in the previous years had, weekly and often
twice weekly, arrived in Dublin, one is amazed that during
the nine months stay in England only four letters from
Matty have been preserved. It is not, simply, that she wrote
letters which, for one reason or another, have been lost or
destroyed, for Dr. Drennan repeatedly reproaches her for
not writing at all. He, for his part, sent long, diffusive
epistles, for the social life at Wem, and the highly intellectual middle class society of his dissenting friends at Liverpool and Chester, interested him enormously, and he

includes constant, if very brief, news of Sarah and the boys, who always sent their love. But it is true that there are no vivid glimpses and stories about Tom for which his sister at Cabin Hill must have yearned. Years ago, when schooling herself to surrender Tom to his parents in Dublin, she had, anticipating the heart-breaking wrench, written thus to Sarah:

> *He owes me nothing . . . every hour he has been with me he has afforded me pleasure, & if he wakes in the night I hear the silver tone of 'turn to me Aunt m'dear—take me in your arms'. When he leaves me all I have to exact (& I think I may) is as particular, parental accounts of him as I have always endeavoured to write.*[18]

Was she, perhaps, a little hurt that now so few details reached her? Or, with the departure of 'her darling' had the grand purpose of her life disappeared, and, without that compelling motive to keep young, had old age, in her sixty-eighth year, swept down upon her with sudden cruelness? She herself mentions being 'lazy' and Dr. Drennan alludes to her having been ill, and, very ominously, to her need of spectacles. Was it, even now, the case that she was bearing the once-dreaded agony of being 'robbed' of her child [p. 7], an agony that could only be endured in silence? These are all surmises, the truth may simply be that with failing sight the old zest for letter-writing had departed—though it revived in later years—and at any rate the paucity of her letters at this time had little effect on Tom. For Tom had now reached the stage, foretold by his Aunt, when his parents and their doings entirely satisfied his needs. He was no longer merely a child: he loved all this travelling about with his father and mother, the new places, and new friends—a sea voyage, a great city, Chester cathedral and much else of which no record has been left. All this completely engrossed his mind, and, utterly unaware of how

immensely Mrs. M'Tier's training had enabled him to take
his place so confidently and with such poise in this new life,
he sailed ahead, as all children do, without a backward
thought for her who had guided him so far. Matty, we may
be certain, understood all this perfectly—it was she who had
sought to lay the foundation of a 'manly' independence, she
who had always wanted Tom to acquit himself easily with
strangers—though it did not make the loss of him any less
poignant. She knew that she must no longer demand a con-
tinuation of his childhood's affection, but she may have felt
that his parents, at any rate, might have been a little more
thoughtful in satisfying her thirst for information.

Be all that as it may, the first of these four surviving
letters from Mrs. M'Tier was written to Dr. Drennan
shortly after his visit to Belfast, and one week before
Christmas 1809, and it begins thus:

*With best wishes for yr. enjoyment of those festivities of
the Season I once enjoyed.* Immediate *answers from this,
not being as necessary as they once were* [one wonders
why], *joined to my increasing laziness, has prevented my
acknowledging your two letters sooner, they are always
acceptable, and particularly saying you are off the Sea,
which does not ever seem to favor you. Your little ones
are as well as you cou'd wish them, on that head, therefore, more cannot be added. To Sarah you may say that
their sweetness of manners, temper, behaviour etc. were
so attractive to company I had staying here that even
Mrs. Mitchell & Mrs. Mateer with their young ladies,
frequently laid down their Novel to listen to their prattle,
which like that of birds, I observe, always is loudest
where there is most sound . . . Sal. improves daily & talks
so much she had made Lenox grave. She is my bedfellow
and will naturally become a favorite, but, I hope neither
Tom nor his Mother will become jealous of an old Aunt.*

*But if* he *wishes to keep his first place, he must write to me, tell me of his companions, favorite schools, and occupations. You say he heads a little company, he should not be placed there, nor anywhere* above *others, but by merit, & nothing could be better for his health & appearance at present than being well drilled by a Sergeant.*[19]

There was never anything effeminate about Matty. The letter concludes with a reference to an article in the *Edinburgh Review* about education, and details about the tenant for the house.

The second letter, written about a month later, is to Tom. It shows clearly how still, in thought, she shares with him all her interests, and must be quoted at length:

*Dear Tom,*

*Tho' you will not write to me, I cannot think it is want of inclination, and sure if your Mama is too busy—your Aunt, or Grandmama, wou'd assist you? Why, when you were but* 4 *years old, I guided your hand to kind remembrance to your Dublin friends, and the one letter I got,\* was so much better wrote that certainly it cou'd not be half so troublesome, besides, I told you, if your watch did not go well, the Man was to take it back.*

*I sent a letter by a private hand to you, as far as Liverpool, which your Papa said you had not got, so there is little encouragement in that mode, & your Mama will be pleased to pay for your letter, when it says her little ones have happily enjoy'd such uninterrupted good health, that there has not been occasion even to open or shut a* back *door on their account these six months. Lennox was very fat, but is not so much so now. Sal is fat, animated & improving. Lenox has got a white scaly substance on his*

---

\* Probably the one mentioned on p. 110, it has not been preserved.

*head which his Aunt hoped to conquer by constant comb-
ing, softening & washing. This has not done, & if your
Mama knows of anything that will do request she will let
me know. There never was a more sickly season in Belfast,
& many attended by three Doctors. Geo. Martin is dead,
& such is the power of good natured Hospitality, that he
is much & generally lamented, even Ld. Donegall cou'd
hardly be prevailed on to go to the Neilson Ball the night
he died. . . .*

*I hope your Father is now at Bath, & finds it either
agreeable or of use, or rather both. He will meet a great
number of old Belfast acquaintances, to such I hope my
sweet Tom will ever go up with a frank, kind address,
this is natural to you, you may recollect how old Mrs.
Houston admired you for it, therefore you may be sure
it was proper. I hope you continue to enter a room always
like a gentleman, never be ashamed of anything, but being
ashamed, for I do not think you will say or do anything
dishonourable, this being in your own Power. How do
you relish school. You are pretty well prepared, & will
not enter a Novice. How does Chess go on, I expect to
play often with you when you return & that you will be
a match for me as I never was good at it, yet still I am
very fond of it, tho' often beat. We have hard frost at
present & I am teaching Len. & Sal Shinnaigh, for which
they appear to have a more promising taste than for
letters. I have been forced to part with Margaret on acct.
of her bad health. She got benefit by your Papa's direc-
tions, but I fear she has water on her chest. Our Theatre
is opened, & Assemblys begun, to neither of which I mean
to be a frequent visitor. The former lost my chief induce-
ment when I parted with my genteel little beau, for you
were, & are yet, at the very time of Life the Stage is
most safely attractive and of great use—to the Boy, afterwards in confirmed Manhood, not as a Youth—when*

*those who have been restricted early pant after it so that*
*they wou'd live in the Theatre, when they show'd be in*
*the Counting House. Farewll my first son (I wish'd you*
*a happy new year on the 1st of it, the date of my last).*

*Your Aunt Drennan joins in the repitition* [sic] *to*
*you, your Mama & brother, with all your new friends.*
*M.M.*[20]

A rather sad and lonely letter! Dr. Drennan's visit to
Bath had been most enjoyable. He was warmly welcomed
by the little colony of former Belfast residents, among them
Matty's old friend Jane Greg. 'She inhabits,' writes the
doctor, 'a very genteel house in a handsome square '[21] Miss
Greg seized the opportunity of Dr. Drennan's visit to send
Matty the present of a bonnet in the very latest fashion—
'white sattin edged with Chenille & made up by the Duchess
of York's Milliner.[22] One hopes that this kind reminder of
a long and scintillating friendship brought cheer to Mrs.
M'Tier. There was also in Bath 'an Elephant who had the
docility of a well taught child, could open a door with his
proboscis, took my glove, waved it round his head, returned
it to my hand, with many other tricks, & I longed to place
Tom & Willy on his Back, along with a Boy who seemed
delighted with the unexpected ride round the Booth where
he was kept.[22]

The third of Mrs. M'Tier's letters is written to Sarah
with continued good reports of Sally and Lennox, 'I have
not one word of news, but mean to go to Belfast tomorrow
for a few Days for some *partys* & by enjoying them, think
in that at least, I have an advantage over my younger
relatives. Tom I think will yet communicate pleasure to me
by taking it in society, & at my fire side—He must *write* his
orders *abt*: his garden whether the ornamental or profitable
is to be studied'.[23]

The fourth, and last of this period, is a gossipy one to
her brother.[24]

The query about Tom's garden is answered, as she requested, by Tom himself, without, it must be admitted very much sign of interest:

> *Dear Aunt*
> *Papa wishes me to tell you how I am. I feel myself very well. You asked me in your letter, would I choose my garden for Pleasure or Profit, I think a little of both will be best. My Grandafther has been very ill but is now a little better. I have no more to say but am ever yours.*
>
> *Thomas Drennan.*[25]

Matty may have thought, and with some justification, that the parents of a boy of nine years old, getting on well at school and enjoying constantly novel experiences in another country, might well have encouraged him to be a little more expansive when writing to his Aunt. If he wrote other letters to her from England none have been preserved.

The family returned to Belfast in May 1810, Mrs. M'Tier having been commissioned to conduct arrangements with the outgoing tenant and to look for servants. For the next eighteen months or so the correspondence consists only of casual notes, all of them from Dr. Drennan, one of which contained 'a thing which I wish to be an exercise for Thomas' memory, wh. Bunting got for his Publication'.[26] This was probably one of the poems which Edward Bunting used in his famous collection of Irish harp music published in 1809, and the remark would indicate that Tom was frequently at Cabin Hill. One imagines that new interests and new ties now bound him to its owner.

Then, with catastrophic suddenness, the sequence of trivial messages is ended by this tragic poem in Dr. Drennan's handwriting:

THOMAS DRENNAN

The Spring returns, but not for Thee, Sweet Boy
    Glides o'er thy grave her animating Breath:
Nature awakes to Light, and Life, and Joy.
    No vernal warmth can pierce the bed of Death.

Beside Thee, blush'd upon the Winter Snows,
    Charming the eye, nor dreading swift decline
At Spring's return, then dy'd the kindred Rose
    As if its tender life were knit with thine.

Clos'd the fair promise of thy opening year:
    Thy early blossoms, thy affections kind;
Soft smiles evolving from a heart sincere;
    And sweet development of beauteous Mind.

A Mind, by manners more than words express'd
    Social, yet secret; resolute tho' mild;
Truth set her seal upon his candid breast;
    And Character was stampt while yet a Child.

I saw my Father pictured in my Son;
    I hop'd his life might glide as smooth away;
And when the calm, sequestered course was run,
    Its Morn and Eve might make one Sabbath Day.

Placid, benign, contemplative, and pure,
    Such was my Father; such wert thou my Child!
Thy Flow'r, I hop'd, would bear his Fruit mature,
    Thy happy Morn attain his Evening mild.

But vain for Thee, our hopes to Heav'n exhal'd
    Though watch'd beside with twice maternal care;
Nor strength of nature, nor of art avail'd
    Nor Stranger's blessing, nor the Poor Man's pray'r.

As from the small remotest Star descends
   The momentary speed of Light divine:
Angelic nature thus with mortal blends,
   And, thus, Thy Spirit may converse with mine.

Where lov'd in life, and humanly ador'd
   Here, let thy Presence shed a sainted grace:
Thy courteous form, to these known walks, restored;
   Be its good Genius still, and sanctify the Place.

*Cabin-Hill,*
*25th February,* 1812.


That is all we know. No record has been left of the last, fatal illness—there was no need to write about it, for Tom's parents and dear 'Aunt Atier' were with him. One of the casual, undated notes already mentioned gives this information: 'Tom is very well, and now has a quilt on his bed and ever since you were here. The Screen is drawn round him every night by Sarah, and I dont think there is any cause for anxiety about him. The reason of his being in that room was the fear of his being disturbed by Lennox. We shall however be happy to see you on Friday and then determine as to the boys as Sarah & you shall think best'. This incident *may* relate to the last illness. If so, it would seem that Sarah and Matty agreed that Thomas should — recuperate — at Cabin Hill, for it was at Cabin Hill that he died.

When, after many months, Mrs. M'Tier and her brother again took up their pens the letters that they wrote contain no mention of an irreparable loss.

There remains, however, a small, plain rectangular crystal locket of exquisite shape and proportions, such as a man would wear on his fob or watch chain. It encloses a little curl of hair and on its simple gold frame this inscription is engraved:

*T.D.  Oh my boy forever dear, forever kind,*
*Once tender friend of my distracted mind.*
*Where he is may I be also.*

Sentimentally phrased, if you like—or so it may seem to a
generation accustomed to the clipped, abbreviated mid-
twentieth century style, but the lines were composed, and
the jewel treasured, by the man who, in a moment of
radiant joy, had written to his wife, not ten years earlier,
concerning this same adored son:

*Don't read this to anyone. Affection is a sacred thing.*

Now, along with that exuberant joy, there was crushing
sorrow.

# Postscript

A little tidying-up is necessary. After Tom's death Dr. Drennan and his family took up residence at Cabin Hill, Mrs. M'Tier moving back to Belfast: the memories attached to the little country cottage were too poignant for her. Dr. Drennan himself died there in 1820, having devoted the last years of his life to founding and editing the *Belfast Magazine*, and taking part with others, in establishing the [Royal] Belfast Academical Institution.

Bereft of those she loved most dearly the close of 'Aunt Atier's' long life was clouded by loneliness, blindness and failing powers. Had Tom lived it was not to be expected that he could have brought to her more than occasional solace. William, at the age of sixteen, entered Trinity College, Dublin. John Swanwick, the little fellow born during the Shropshire holiday, followed in his father's footsteps in so far as he became a doctor and wrote some poetry. Sally became the wife of John Andrews of Comber, Co. Down. It was Lennox, always quiet and gentle, and about whom we know little, who, to some extent, comforted Mrs. M'Tier's last years. She died in 1837, aged ninety-four.

# References

*Abbreviations*: D.L.=Drennan Letters.
L.S.=Dr. Drennan's letters to his wife.

## Chapter I: His first two years, *page* 1

| 1 | D.L. | No. | 918 | 7 | D.L. | No. | 987 |
|---|---|---|---|---|---|---|---|
| 2 | ,, | ,, | 927 | 8 | ,, | ,, | 1,015 |
| 3 | ,, | ,, | 937 | 9 | ,, | ,, | 1,021 |
| 4 | ,, | ,, | 940 | 10 | ,, | ,, | 1,013 |
| 5 | ,, | ,, | 978 | 11 | ,, | ,, | 1,028 |
| 6 | ,, | ,, | 1,060 | | | | |

## Chapter II: Two years old, *page* 11

| 1 | D.L. | No. | 1,035 | 16 | D.L. | No. | 1,066 |
|---|---|---|---|---|---|---|---|
| 2 | ,, | ,, | 1,032 | 17 | ,, | ,, | 1,073 |
| 3 | ,, | ,, | 1,036 | 18 | ,, | ,, | 1,089 |
| 4 | ,, | ,, | 1,037 | 19 | ,, | ,, | 1,090 |
| 5 | ,, | ,, | 1,065 | 20 | ,, | ,, | 1,084 |
| 6 | ,, | ,, | 1,037 | 21 | ,, | ,, | 1,054 |
| 7 | ,, | ,, | 1,047 | 22 | ,, | ,, | 1,066 |
| 8 | ,, | ,, | 1,038 | 23 | L.S. | | |
| 9 | ,, | ,, | 1,048 | 24 | D.L. | No. | 1,078 |
| 9a | ,, | ,, | 1,054 | 25 | ,, | ,, | 1,107 |
| 10 | ,, | ,, | 1,053 | 26 | ,, | ,, | 1,048 |
| 11 | ,, | ,, | 1,055 | 27 | ,, | ,, | 1,071 |
| 12 | ,, | ,, | 1,054 | 28 | ,, | ,, | 1,076 |
| 13 | ,, | ,, | 1,060 | 29 | ,, | ,, | 1,077 |
| 14 | ,, | ,, | 1,061 | 30 | ,, | ,, | 1,075a |
| 15 | ,, | ,, | 1,062 | 31 | ,, | ,, | 1,088 |

| 32 | D.L. | No. 1,057 | 35 | D.L. | No. 1,078 |
|----|------|-----------|----|------|-----------|
| 33 | " | " 1,086 | 36 | " | " 1,086 |
| 34 | " | " 1,093 | | | |

## Chapter III: Three years old, *page* 29

| 1 | D.L. | No. 1,096 | 24 | D.L. | No. 1,105 |
|---|------|-----------|----|------|-----------|
| 2 | " | " 1,105 | 25 | " | " 1,129 |
| 3 | " | " 1,111 | 26 | " | " 1,130 |
| 4 | " | " 1,109 | 27 | " | " 1,131 |
| 5 | " | " 1,101 | 28 | " | " 1,132 |
| 6 | " | " 1,110 | 29 | " | " 1,133 |
| 7 | Quoted in Introduction, facsimile reproduction of 1766 edition of *Goody Two-Shoes*, Griffith & Farran. | | 30 | " | " 1,136 |
| | | | 31 | " | " 1,139 |
| | | | 32 | " | " 1,144 |
| | | | 33 | " | " 1,146 |
| | | | 34 | " | " 1,150 |
| 8 | D.L. | No. 1,126 | 35 | " | " 1,118 |
| 9 | " | " 1,127 | 36 | " | " 1,110 |
| 10 | " | " 1,003 | 37 | " | " 1,179 |
| 11 | " | " 1,122 | 38 | Quoted Georgian Chronicle, p. 72. B. Rodgers: Methuen. By permission. | |
| 12 | " | " 1,118 | | | |
| 13 | " | " 1,123 | | | |
| 14 | " | " 1,121 | | | |
| 15 | " | " 1,073 | 39 | D.L. | No. 1,096 |
| 16 | " | " 1,094 | 40 | " | " 1,137 |
| 17 | " | " 1,107 | 41 | " | " 1,149 |
| 18 | " | " 1,140 | 42 | " | " 1,150 |
| 19 | " | " 1,123 | 43 | " | " 1,151 |
| 20 | " | " 1,091 | 44 | " | " 1,152 |
| 21 | " | " 1,159 | 45 | " | " 1,167 |
| 22 | " | " 1,160 | 46 | " | " 1,166 |
| 23 | " | " 1,161 | 47 | " | " 1,167 |

## Chapter IV: Four years old, *page 58*

| | | | | | | | |
|---|---|---|---|---|---|---|---|
| 1 | D.L. | No. | 1,168 | 15 | D.L. | No. | 1,183 |
| 2 | L.S. | | | 16 | L.S. | | |
| 3 | D.L. | No. | 1,169 | 17 | D.L. | No. | 1,189 |
| 4 | ,, | ,, | 1,170 | 18 | ,, | ,, | 1,199 |
| 5 | ,, | ,, | 1,172 | 19 | ,, | ,, | 1,202 |
| 6 | ,, | ,, | 1,170 | 20 | ,, | ,, | 1,201 |
| 7 | ,, | ,, | 1,173 | 21 | ,, | ,, | 1,205 |
| 8 | ,, | ,, | 1,171 | 22 | ,, | ,, | 1,210 |
| 9 | ,, | ,, | 1,174 | 23 | ,, | ,, | 1,212 |
| 10 | ,, | ,, | 1,172 | 24 | ,, | ,, | 1,212a |
| 11 | ,, | ,, | 1,181 | 25 | ,, | ,, | 1,221 |
| 12 | ,, | ,, | 1,180 | 26 | ,, | ,, | 1,225 |
| 13 | ,, | ,, | 1,181 | 27 | ,, | ,, | 1,226 |
| 14 | ,, | ,, | 1,182 | 28 | ,, | ,, | 1,232 |

## Chapter V: Five years old, *page 79*

| | | | | | | | |
|---|---|---|---|---|---|---|---|
| 1 | D.L. | No. | 1,240 | 14 | D.L. | No. | 1,287 |
| 2 | ,, | ,, | 1,246 | 15 | ,, | ,, | 1,249 |
| 3 | ,, | ,, | 1,314 | 16 | ,, | ,, | 1,253 |
| 4 | ,, | ,, | 1,313 | 17 | ,, | ,, | 1,249 |
| 5 | ,, | ,, | 1,289 | 18 | ,, | ,, | 1,289 |
| 6 | ,, | ,, | 1,296 | 19 | ,, | ,, | 1,296 |
| 7 | In the possession of the Misses Duffin. | | | 20 | ,, | ,, | 1,228 |
| | | | | 21 | ,, | ,, | 1,283 |
| 8 | D.L. | No. | 1,301 | 22 | ,, | ,, | 1,291 |
| 9 | ,, | ,, | 1,302 | 23 | ,, | ,, | 1,254 |
| 10 | ,, | ,, | 1,309 | 24 | ,, | ,, | 1,257 |
| 11 | ,, | ,, | 1,253 | 25 | ,, | ,, | 1,258 |
| 12 | ,, | ,, | 1,253 | 26 | ,, | ,, | 1,264 |
| 13 | ,, | ,, | 1,261 | 27 | ,, | ,, | 1,261 |

| | | | | | | | |
|---|---|---|---|---|---|---|---|
| 28 | D.L. | No. | 1,263 | 37 | D.L. | No. | 1,292 |
| 29 | ,, | ,, | 1,276 | 38 | ,, | ,, | 1,296 |
| 30 | ,, | ,, | 1,277 | 39 | ,, | ,, | 1,297 |
| 31 | ,, | ,, | 1,281 | 40 | ,, | ,, | 1,298 |
| 32 | ,, | ,, | 1,283 | 41 | ,, | ,, | 1,299 |
| 33 | ,, | ,, | 1,284 | 42 | ,, | ,, | 1,300 |
| 34 | ,, | ,, | 1,306 | 43 | ,, | ,, | 1,313 |
| 35 | ,, | ,, | 1,283 | 44 | ,, | ,, | 1,311 |
| 36 | ,, | ,, | 1,283 | 45 | ,, | ,, | 1,313 |

CHAPTER VI: Six to ten years old, *page* 100

| | | | | | | | |
|---|---|---|---|---|---|---|---|
| 1 | D.L. | No. | 1,319 | 13 | D.L. | No. | 1,353 |
| 2 | ,, | ,, | 1,324 | 14 | ,, | ,, | 1,363 |
| 3 | L.S. | | | 15 | ,, | ,, | 1,371 |
| 4 | D.L. | No. | 1,332 | 16 | ,, | ,, | 1,364 |
| 5 | ,, | ,, | 1,338 | 17 | ,, | ,, | 1,361 |
| 6 | ,, | ,, | 1,343 | 18 | ,, | ,, | 1,103 |
| 7 | ,, | ,, | 1,349 | 19 | ,, | ,, | 1,362 |
| 8 | ,, | ,, | 1,350 | 20 | ,, | ,, | 1,365 |
| 9 | ,, | ,, | 1,351 | 21 | ,, | ,, | 1,366 |
| 10 | Quoted *Children's* | | | 22 | ,, | ,, | 1,368 |
| | *Books in England*, p. | | | 23 | ,, | ,, | 1,367 |
| | 191. Harvey Darton. | | | 24 | ,, | ,, | 1,369 |
| | By permission, C.U.P. | | | 25 | ,, | ,, | 1,370 |
| 11 | D.L. | No. | 1,351 | 26 | ,, | ,, | 1,377 |
| 12 | ,, | ,, | 1,352 | | | | |

# Index